6

Recovery
Continues

Recovery Continues

SA Literature

Grateful acknowledgement is made for permission to reprint the following:

Excerpts from *Alcoholics Anonymous*. Copyright © 1976 by Alcoholics Anonymous World Services, Inc. Reprinted by permission of Alcoholics Anonymous World Services, Inc.

Excerpts from *Twelve Steps and Twelve Traditions*. Copyright © 1953 by Alcoholics Anonymous World Services, Inc. Reprinted by permission of Alcoholics Anonymous World Services, Inc.

ISBN 0-9622887-2-1

Recovery continues . . .
This is the marvel of
the grace of God
not only in personal lives
but also in our fellowship.

Contents

Foreword

The various papers included here continue the story of recovery first described in our book *Sexaholics Anonymous*. Most of these originated as personal inventories of common events in day-to-day living. In a process continuing from 1984 to the present, and based on fellowship response, the articles were made available from the Central Office as "loose literature in process." As announced in the March 1987 and May 1988 issues of *Essay* (the SA newsletter), these have since been edited and are now bound together for the first time in this form. They are arranged in the order in which they first appeared. Most of the pieces have undergone minor editorial changes. Some have been substantially revised.

"We lead with our weakness, bearing witness to the truth of our own experience – the only viable message we have." Recovery continues. This is the marvel of the grace of God not only in personal lives but also in our fellowship.

The Twelve Steps of Alcoholics Anonymous

1. We admitted we were powerless over alcohol – that our lives had become unmanageable. **2.** Came to believe that a Power greater than ourselves could restore us to sanity. **3.** Made a decision to turn our will and our lives over to the care of God *as we understood Him.* **4.** Made a searching and fearless moral inventory of ourselves. **5.** Admitted to God, to ourselves, and to another human being the exact nature of our wrongs. **6.** Were entirely ready to have God remove all these defects of character. **7.** Humbly asked Him to remove our shortcomings. **8.** Made a list of all persons we had harmed, and became willing to make amends to them all. **9.** Made direct amends to such people wherever possible, except when to do so would injure them or others. **10.** Continued to take personal inventory and when we were wrong promptly admitted it. **11.** Sought through prayer and meditation to improve our conscious contact with God *as we understood Him, pr*aying only for knowledge of His will for us and the power to carry that out. **12.** Having had a spiritual awakening as the result of these Steps, we tried to carry this message to alcoholics, and to practice these principles in all our affairs.

The Twelve Traditions of Alcoholics Anonymous

1. Our common welfare should come first; personal recovery depends upon AA unity. **2.** For our group purpose there is but one ultimate authority – a loving God as He may express Himself in our group conscience. Our leaders are but trusted servants; they do not govern. **3.** The only requirement for AA membership is a desire to stop drinking. **4.** Each group should be autonomous except in matters affecting other groups or AA as a whole. **5.** Each group has but one primary purpose – to carry its message to the alcoholic who still suffers. **6.** An AA group ought never endorse, finance, or lend the AA name to any related facility or outside enterprise, lest problems of money, property, and prestige divert us from our primary purpose. **7.** Every AA group ought to be fully self-supporting, declining outside contributions. **8.** Alcoholics Anonymous should remain forever nonprofessional, but our service centers may employ special workers. **9.** AA, as such, ought never be organized; but we may create service boards or committees directly responsible to those they serve. **10.** Alcoholics Anonymous has no opinion on outside issues; hence the AA name ought never be drawn into public controversy. **11.** Our public relations policy is based on attraction rather than promotion; we need always maintain personal anonymity at the level of press, radio, and films. **12.** Anonymity is the spiritual foundation of all our Traditions, ever reminding us to place principles before personalities.

The Twelve Steps of Sexaholics Anonymous

1. We admitted that we were powerless over lust – that our lives had become unmanageable.

2. Came to believe that a Power greater than ourselves could restore us to sanity.

3. Made a decision to turn our will and our lives over to the care of God as we understood Him.

4. Made a searching and fearless moral inventory of ourselves.

5. Admitted to God, to ourselves, and to another human being the exact nature of our wrongs.

6. Were entirely ready to have God remove all these defects of character.

7. Humbly asked Him to remove our shortcomings.

8. Made a list of all persons we had harmed, and became willing to make amends to them all.

9. Made direct amends to such people wherever possible, except when to do so would injure them or others.

10. Continued to take personal inventory and when we were wrong promptly admitted it.

11. Sought through prayer and meditation to improve our conscious contact with God as we understood Him, praying only for knowledge of His will for us and the power to carry that out.

12. Having had a spiritual awakening as the result of these Steps, we tried to carry this message to sexaholics and to practice these principles in all our affairs.

Reprinted for adaptation with permission of Alcoholics Anonymous World Services, Inc.

The Twelve Traditions of Sexaholics Anonymous

1. Our common welfare should come first; personal recovery depends on SA unity.

2. For our group purpose there is but one ultimate authority – a loving God as He may express Himself in our group conscience. Our leaders are but trusted servants; they do not govern.

3. The only requirement for membership is a desire to stop lusting and become sexually sober.

4. Each group should be autonomous except in matters affecting other groups or Sexaholics Anonymous as a whole.

5. Each group has but one primary purpose – to carry its message to the sexaholic who still suffers.

6. An SA group ought never endorse, finance, or lend the SA name to any related facility or outside enterprise, lest problems of money, property, and prestige divert us from our primary purpose.

7. Every SA group ought to be fully self-supporting, declining outside contributions.

8. Sexaholics Anonymous should remain forever nonprofessional, but our service centers may employ special workers.

9. SA, as such, ought never be organized; but we may create service boards or committees directly responsible to those they serve.

10. Sexaholics Anonymous has no opinion on outside issues; hence the SA name ought never be drawn into public controversy.

11. Our public relations policy is based on attraction rather than promotion; we need always maintain personal anonymity at the level of press, radio, films, and TV.

12. Anonymity is the spiritual foundation of all our traditions, ever reminding us to place principles before personalities.

Reprinted for adaptation with permission of Alcoholics Anonymous World Services, Inc.

Masturbation and Sexual Sobriety

Why do I find it necessary to include freedom from any form of sex with myself as part of my sexual sobriety?

Masturbation for me means escape from reality. It is a mood-altering, mind-altering experience – an addictive drug. In my experience, this escape took two forms. When I first began masturbating, it was not connected with any mental imagery. The physical sensation helped blank out my mind – a mindless retreat from reality. I would lose total contact with the world, others, and myself. Escape. It was a way of blocking out my inner distress and the distress of my environment. It wasn't long, however, before masturbation took on the second and, for me, the permanent form of being driven by images. I would use pictures or conjure from mind or memory an imaginary sex partner. This second form may have been trying to fill the emotional deficit in my life; a surrogate Connection. What I didn't realize was that conjuring up a sex partner from within seems to be a division of my self. Both of these forms of masturbation – with or without images – were escape from *me*. Each act drove me further into that dreadful isolation that is one of the hallmarks of our sexaholism. I was slowly losing me.

In masturbation as an adult (having by then added marriage, affairs, one-night stands, and prostitution), I was still nourishing in my mind and heart the attitudes and actions my lust would like to make real. Thus, all the features of my diseased sexual behavior are present in masturbation: mood-alteration, self-splitting, and losing of self.

Masturbation for me is the same as my acting out with others; the presence of a sexual partner was merely another extension of autoeroticism.

Masturbation lights the fuse, sets me up so I lose control again – the "first drink" that gets me drunk and out of control, unable to stop.

> *Another member says, "I find myself drinking before I ever start masturbating. The first drink is the first lust thought I consciously entertain. Lust acts as a narcotic in my bloodstream so that I have to masturbate. I've heard it said in AA that taking a drink is the last thing I do on a slip. And masturbation is the last thing I do on a slip. Masturbation is the result; lust is the underlying problem."*

Thank God there's a remedy for both!

1982, rev. 7/85, 1/90

Defects Continued–Hostility

One day at work, I began wondering why, when in the presence of hostile people, I got hostile feelings inside. Why did I have this bad feeling just because they did?

At a noon AA meeting I talked about it. The very next man who shared identified strongly; he had even killed a man once in a hostile reaction. It was easy to see what hostility was in his life; he confessed to being powerless over it most of the time. It's so easy to see what's wrong with others, isn't it?

Others shared, and I left the meeting to get back to work, feeling great relief. I finally had the answer; the reason I felt hostile when confronted with hostility was because I *am* hostile, in the sense that I have hostility, and it comes out on occasion. It doesn't matter how, why, or when I got that way. I was able to see and accept it as I had, years ago, accepted I was a sex drunk. I use hostility as a drug; it does something for me. I get a true "hit" off it; it has a mood-altering effect. It gets into my bloodstream and changes me.

That admission – my own powerlessness over hostility – became the key to my progressive victory over hostility. All I have to do is own and surrender it, and I'm free. Of course, that's easier said than done, and often the feelings linger or come back, and I have to surrender again. So now, every morning and evening, when I surrender my lust to the One who bears it for me, I do the same with my hostility. I give up to Him my negative attitude toward others *and* my lust one day at a time, one event at a time, because I can't live with the pain it causes me and can't cure it.

Of course, temptations to get a "high" off my negative force occur as they did before: the slow driver ahead, the guy at work who's negative and defensive, the secretary with the clever put-down. . . I think I might even be going through hostility withdrawal, the same kind of symptoms as lust withdrawal: heightened awareness of it, disguised and undisguised; being a little edgy; and so on. And is it being tested! But I'd rather be going through this process than stay where I was.

Now I have a choice. I can surrender my bad feeling on the spot, give it up to Him, let Him bear it for me . . . and I'm free! What a beautiful freedom! I don't have to stay with any of those negative feelings anymore! I have a choice!

Many of us were raised in an environment that radiated hostility – overt or covert. We were powerless over that polluted atmosphere. However, I see now that I did have a choice in my attitude *toward* that environment, but I chose to go negative and bury the feeling so deep inside that it was not apparent to me or others – until, that is, it would flash out like lightning and try to strike somebody dead. I would keep the negative force sedated with my other drugs, sex and lust; but over the long haul, I was absolutely powerless over my resentment *and* my lust and sex.

For me, the key to victory and recovery is to come out of denial and see, acknowledge, and surrender the temptation to go negative every time it tries to slip through the door into my soul and run amuck. Surrender is now one of the most beautiful words in the world to me; it's the Key. It's a dying, each time, but on the other side of it there's new birth. Each time I get that negative feeling now, instead of denying I'm hostile, I let it become just another means of making the real Connection. And slowly, over time, the temptation to "take a drink" of hostility is less and less. There's increased comfort inside myself and a little more freedom to live comfortably with others.

5 September 1983, rev. 7/85, 1/90

Another Look at Lust

I'm sitting in the audience of a town meeting, listening to presentations by various groups, when a woman I've known professionally sits next to me and starts trying to connect with me. As she comments on what is being said, she is reaching for eye contact, and when she gets it, tries to hold me fast in that contact, to pull me in. I feel I am being forced against my will and desire. The attraction – if that's what it is – is not mutual, but she seems obsessed with it.

Pretty soon, however, I find myself responding to her – just to be polite, or so I think. What will she think if I keep on ignoring her? Besides, she's a great help in understanding what's going on with the presentations; she is extremely well informed.

Then, she makes shoulder contact, and this continues with the running commentary and eye-pull, to get me to respond. At every eye contact she hangs onto me hungrily as long as she can with each look, not wanting to lose me again.

I did not think about leaving or calling on God's presence during this encounter because lust was not involved – I thought. I was actually annoyed. What I did not realize was that I was being tempted to take a drink of *another* drug – losing myself in her.

I began to be tempted to let myself go and give in to her. I was getting some kind of satisfaction from her desire for me, and the more I responded, the more I wanted to respond, the more attractive she became, and the more I wanted to be taken captive. I found the fleeting fantasy arising to let go and lose myself in her. And I had created the need for this within myself.

This kind of *taking* – trying to pull someone in with or without their consent – is the kind of thing I had supposed was peculiar to us males. There is force involved, not necessarily physical, with or without any signal or willingness from the other person. And the force springs from demand, from an obsessive "intense desire." But here it was coming from a woman, and *I* was on the receiving end, experiencing what I thought would have been a woman's reaction!

Passive lust wants to be taken in by another – to give in to the desire of another; to be overwhelmed so I won't be responsible. I want to "let myself go." This may be what I used to experience as "falling in love." The word "falling" describes it perfectly! I give up control or lose control and fall into that force-field of desire and dependency.

Even when the force-field of desire is generated by the other person, it's really the void in *me* and *my* desire that causes me to fall. There may even be something within me – conscious or subconscious – signalling the other person to turn their desire onto me.

Thus, lust can be active or passive; it wants to take or it wants to be taken. In either case, it seems to spring from spiritual emptiness and an inner demand to fill the void with a substitute for God.

What we commonly call *lust* and what we experience as dependency or relationship addiction may really be two sides of the same coin.

The remedy for both my active and passive lust is to acknowledge my powerlessness and surrender it to God; to let myself feel the emptiness and fill the void with God and giving to others. The Steps in action. There are times, such as this incident, when I've been without defense against the first drink, when, at the time, I don't even recognize what's going on. At such times, the only thing that has saved me has been the "insurance policy" of daily surrender and trying to work this program in all areas of my life.

14 September 1984, rev. 1/90

The Resentment-Lust Connection

My wife was cooking a special breakfast, and I made the remark in passing that she should turn on the exhaust fan to keep the smell of bacon from smelling up the whole house. The incident triggered resentment, even though it was repressed. In this instance, there was no outburst or even anger, but there was something insidious in my tone. I disconnected from her, withdrawing into the prison-house of the self, retreating into that "safe" isolation of being *apart*. It was a quiet severing of the bond. Sometimes I can also detect the feeling of wanting to punish the other person or a feeling that says, "Well, just for that, I'll deprive you of myself!" *She* doesn't seem to disconnect from me when she fails to turn on the exhaust fan, but I disconnect from her. Maddening!

In the past, this scene would have been played with high-decibel vociferation on my part; but with or without the fireworks, it's the same inner script. The negative spiritual action comes from the deepest core of my being as an attitude that sets me against the other person. I disconnect and hit back, even if it's in a subtle, indirect way. Such behavior tells the whole story about me; this is what I really am!

I walked on past the kitchen out to the study and, within seconds, found myself in a fantasy conversation with a former lover. In my mind I talked with her on the phone, angling for a get-together and enticing her with what I knew she wanted to hear – something that would trigger her lust. Mind you, that very morning I had had a dream with very warm and loving feelings for my wife in a true-union setting.

So here's the question: Does even a "minor" negative attitude (I didn't voice anger or make a scene) make me more susceptible to lust? Apparently so. I disconnect from someone; I want to connect with lust (or some other false connection). Cause and effect. I disconnect from a person; I want to reconnect with the *super*-natural fix that always offered instant CONNECTION. Fusion instead of union. In severing the real bond, I want to connect with the unreal, and the lust connection seems *super*-real. It's always lying in wait, even though I discovered long ago that it was not only not real but self-destructive – that it always robbed me of life instead of giving me the life it promised.

Why is this whole disconnection-resentment game destructive? Because when I sever from Person, I'm severing from God. The two always seem to go together; I can't do damage to one without doing damage to the other. Also, this kind of severing is a conscious attitude *against* another, and thus an inner act of violence. But the only one inside me is *me,* so that inner violence damages *me.* That's why I feel bad when I do what is wrong.

When I became aware of that lust fantasy playing in my head and gave it up to God, saying I wanted no part of it, I was freed of its presence and power. I thank God that I have such a choice today! But I was still incomplete. The job wasn't finished because I was still disconnected from my wife. And the only way to change that was to reconnect. But I didn't want to; I wanted to stay sealed off in that prison-house I'd pulled back into. I preferred the isolation that my spiritual action had created, and I was stuck in that moment of dread and indecision. I was disturbed; bad feelings inside. "I don't *want* to make it right. I just can't!" I was saying to myself. The hardest thing in the world for me is to go back to the person and make it right. I'd rather die! But I *have* to make it right – to live.

So, in an act of *positive* "violence" – doing violence to my old nature and dying to it – I forced myself to reconnect with my wife. A few casual words and a touch – again in passing. But that's all it took, *and I was whole again*.

We are truly so very fortunate; our dis-ease forces us to clean up our act. I simply can't get away with disconnecting for very long anymore; the result is immediate discomfort and liability to lust. I can't stay sober and free without dealing with my negative disconnecting temperament in the same way I deal with my lust: surrendering to my powerlessness over it, giving it up to God, and asking Him to take it. *And then making it right with the other person. Reconnecting.* This brings instant healing from all kinds of bad feelings, healing that is priceless, unfailing, and absolutely free!

6 December 1984, rev. 1/90

Abstinence in Marriage

B y the time most of us had entered the program, lust had had a field day. In recovery, we come to see how much we were possessed and controlled by lust. Lust poisoned us and it poisoned others. The marriage bed was no exception. How could we be infected with lust and *not* have it affect relations with our spouses? Many married newcomers to SA have found that it is extremely difficult, if not impossible, to separate sex from lust when they are trying to get sober initially. How many times have we heard something like

> *"Well, I had sex with the wife again, like we'd been doing, and it felt wrong, as though I'd had a slip."*

What has facilitated withdrawal from lust, for those married members who have tried it in the right spirit, is a period of voluntary sexual abstinence. Taking sex out of the marriage for a time also helps us see what there really is (or is not) in the marriage. If sex is the only thing holding it together, there's probably not much there. When some of us come into the program, our marriages are in such a state that abstinence seems the only wise thing to do. This allows

---

This piece was formerly titled "Sexual Detox."

the spouse to recover from the trauma of disclosure, hopeless despair, anger, and possibly even from lust itself. Plus, it allows the sexaholic to recover from the toxic effects and associations of lust.

Some married members have gone through months and even years of this "detoxification" so readily and to such advantage that later in sobriety they have repeated the mutual abstinence in order to inventory and improve their lives and marriage. Those doing so have been surprised by the discovery that sex is indeed optional, even in the marriage, when surrendered freely, and that great benefits can accrue to the relationship.

Sex in the marriage of a recovering sexaholic can mask either the true measure of lust or its gradual reintroduction. In marital sex, lust can hide in cunning and baffling ways. It tries to find a way back in without our realizing it. Abstinence has a way of uncovering this and bringing it to our attention so we can take steps to reinforce the true Connection.

However, periods of sexual abstinence in marriage can be fruitless or even counterproductive if not accompanied by increased activity with the Steps to surrender lust and taking the actions of love to improve relations with our spouse and others. And we must always be careful of the feelings of the spouse, who may interpret abstinence as a message that they are no longer wanted. Often, our relationship was centered on sexual activity, and it is possible that sexual disconnection may initiate a crisis or uncover problems in the spouse. Therefore, proposed abstinence should be discussed beforehand and, during such periods, the sexaholic should *increase* his or her nonsexual contact, communication, and caring. Abstinence can thus become a precious opportunity for enhancing the bond of spiritual union.

January 1985, rev. 1/90

Self-Awareness and Sexual Dreams

Recovering from the obsession of lust is an amazing journey into self. We used to have to run from this self; now we get to know and accept ourselves. With the pain of self-awareness comes the blessing of the Remedy and healing. And with healing comes an increased willingness to take responsibility for the self in all its manifestations. It's been surprising and most interesting to discover that my self, at any and all of its levels, is *me*.

The Progressive Revelation of the Self

The first layer or level of the self the sober sexaholic in recovery seems to become aware of and begin to get victory over is lust. The typical reaction is, "I had no idea I was so full of lust until I stopped acting out." On initial surrender and withdrawal, we become aware of lust thoughts previously below the level of awareness. Lust was so much a part of our inner world that we had to step outside it in order to see it. Lust was so much the air we breathed that

---

This piece was formerly titled "Sobriety and the Subconscious" or "Sobriety and the Self."

16

we weren't aware of it. Like fish out of water, and suddenly–! There seems to be no better way of seeing the power lust has over us than to get sexually sober. Once we stop the acting out – or try stopping – lust becomes apparent, and what was previously operating below the surface hits us full-face. Awareness of the depth of our lust brings the first step in the marvelous adventure into the deepening awareness of the self. This is based on willingness to start seeing ourselves as we really are. Withdrawal leads us into the first level of spiritual awareness.

However, awareness of lust brings distress, so much distress that we either are driven back to lust or go on with God. Perhaps this is why so many of us leave the program at this first stage. We feel the pain and emptiness but have nothing with which to ease and fill it. "The only way to be free of it was to do it." What a tragic lostness!

The next level we begin to see is opened up through the next defect that surfaces. Often this is resentment or its kin. When I first became aware of resentment in early sobriety, it was something new. I hadn't known such feelings before! Of course not; they had been below the level of awareness, covered over by my drugs. The fact that these negative feelings broke through every once in a while had to be an accident, or the fault of others. If we begin honestly to face the first defect that surfaces and get victory over it, we gradually develop the capacity to see more, and then the next defect rears its head. Maybe it's one of those blood brothers of resentment: anger; hostility; or a judging, condemning, vindictive, unforgiving spirit. Negative feelings toward others. Not *all* others; just those who are obviously so "wrong and bad." Right? Our self-blindness is so cunning. The point is, as we enlarge our capacity to see ourselves as we really are, one defect at a time, the awareness of self deepens, and we enlarge our capacity and hunger for rightness and God.

If I say I have no wrong I deceive myself.

Over the months and years – if we stay sober and walk in the light – we slowly become aware of layer after layer of our unsoundness and the discomfort it causes. We use the Steps and fellowship to continue treating it. This can be very slow in coming. Sometimes it takes a few years to begin to achieve this awareness. And some people seem unable to do so. It's called "trudging the Road of Happy Destiny." But with the trudging come the joy and the freedom and the growth into what we were created for.

If we were to try to summarize what is operating in this odyssey into the self, it might look like this:

- Starting with lust, we increasingly see more of our defective selves.
- As each new defect becomes apparent, we acknowledge what we see. (That's where others in the fellowship come in; we have to have them to acknowledge it *to*.)
- We see our powerlessness over each defect.
- We surrender each defect and send it away to God.
- We get progressive victory over each defect.
- Increasingly we get freedom to be what we are (defective) *because* we have the Remedy. Acceptance of the self increases.
- This enlarges our capacity, need, and hunger for God.
- We have greater fulfillment – union and fellowship with our God and others.
- All this means a growing willingness to see and surrender defects, a growing hunger for rightness and God, and continued deepening of the awareness of self, recovery, and growth.

When we look at our recovery from this perspective, we see that just as the whole person was involved in our sexaholism, the whole person – as progressively revealed – must be involved in our recovery.

The Effect of Self-Awareness on Our Relations with Others

Deepening awareness and progressive victory over our own defects seem to bring an increasing willingness to surrender our negative feelings toward others. And these negative feelings become just another of our continuing compelling needs not only to surrender and connect with God but also to be a channel of His peace to the very people we would negate.

This healing process toward others is part of what makes fellowship with those who are in recovery so precious. We lead with our weakness. We bring our wrongs out into the light. We see the weakest aspects of ourselves and others around the table. And when we share together in surrender and obedience to God, making amends as necessary, we are united with one another. It creates identification with and acceptance of each other at the deepest level, and this leads to love for one another – a spring of living water welling up and flowing out to those still thirsting for that which satisfies.

If we choose not to live in this way, we hinder group fellowship at the deeper level. We may even cause the group to remain at one level or slowly decay.

This may also be why it is best not to take notes in meetings on what is said or on what we wish to say. Doing so inhibits our learning how to listen, talk, respond, and act spontaneously. Our goal is to awaken and deepen the progressively purified intuitive side of our nature and thereby *connect* with the others present in a very real way – being *part of*, instead of coming *at* people from our isolating intellect, knowledge, or self-obsession. And when we connect with each other on this cleansed intuitive level, we are learning how to connect with God.

Meditation

Meditation in the right spirit can be part of this process of increasing awareness of the self and enlarging our capacity for true union with others and God. And when coupled with prayer for others, it can greatly add to our usefulness and peace of mind. (See Step Eleven in *Sexaholics Anonymous*.)

However, a word of caution is in order. We bring to meditation what we are as a person. If I come to meditation while harboring resentment or an unforgiving spirit, or come with a spirit filled with the world's noise or the noise of my own disorder, what can I expect? Meditation can promote recovery only if honesty is at work and there is surrender to God commensurate with that honesty. We can meditate while still blind to the truth about ourselves. Meditation is not a badge of spiritual progress in and of itself. Anyone can meditate, just as anyone can pray. The true reality of ourselves becomes more clearly apparent in the light of other recovering persons around the meeting table, another compelling reason why we cannot recover alone.

Dreams

As awareness of the self slowly deepens, we increasingly learn to take responsibility for *all* of ourselves, including our dreams. Dreams can be a mirror into which we look to see parts of ourselves we may still be hiding from, a benign way of facing ourselves. It is as though part of us is sitting across the table in a meeting and gently holding up a mirror into which we are invited to look. We may not understand all of our dreams; we don't have to. But we can learn to trust God for help and know that our dreams are involved in the process of recovery just as our waking self is.

It seems that our lust can tempt us during sleep just as lust tempts us during waking hours. Increasingly we are finding that we can surrender lust in sleep as we do when awake. We *can* have the choice. If we want it. We might think that such a thing is impossible, but our SA experience proves that we can progressively learn to do this.

When I've had dreams with erotic content, I've been forced to acknowledge there may be part of me that's unsurrendered. If I don't, I'm asking for trouble. There's always a price to be paid for unsurrendered lust. I'm forced to own up to it, bring it to the light of others, and send it away, praying for God to fill that defective need with His own presence. Whether I like to admit it or not, *my dreams are me,* and I must start seeing and taking responsibility for what they are telling me.

Sexual Dreams

The foregoing look at our progressive self-awareness in recovery puts the subject of sexual dreams in proper perspective. By sexual dreams we mean cases in which an individual is aware of having sex in a dream. We can only speak for ourselves – not the rest of the world out there – and we are beginning to learn some things in SA. However, we do not presume to be any kind of authority on sex, nocturnal emissions, or sexual dreams or to offer any medical advice.

It might seem logical that upon initial withdrawal from sex, some men might experience nocturnal emissions, with or without dreams. And, of course, some of us do. Some women members say there is an aspect of this with which they too can identify. It might be argued that the person is habituated to having sex every so often, and when that doesn't take place, the body itself does it automatically. However, many single men testify to going through initial withdrawal from sex with no such experience, and married members report going into voluntary abstinence on different occasions without having sexual dreams. Some married men and women even speak of a "vacation" from sex as a welcome relief. There is no evidence from SA members that says sexual dreams are necessary or unavoidable.

Our experience in recovery is telling us sexaholics that *whenever lust is operating,* a demand for sex is created that must eventually be fulfilled, either at the conscious or subconscious level. How many times have we heard in meetings of those who have flirted with lust during the day – television, "lust hits" off people, or glancing through a magazine perhaps – and then have had a sexual dream?

Also, there are members who abstain from sex with themselves and others and yet have sexual dreams regularly, sometimes as often as they used to have sex. As these members bring this to the light of the group month after month and a pattern emerges, they often begin asking themselves whether in fact there is still something unsurrendered.

The fact is, there are many sober sexaholics of both sexes, single and married, who do not experience sexual activity in sleep or dreams. And there are members who have experienced dream sex and dream lust who have come through to surrender, victory, and freedom.

Many ask whether having had a sexual dream constitutes a lapse in sexual sobriety. This is ultimately the individual's decision. As concerned members, we may question that decision, but we do not *declare* a person either sober or not sober. When other members in a group listen to a person who keeps coming back playing the same broken record, and these other members testify to the truth of their own experiences, this light will hopefully penetrate the defenses of those who are still unsurrendered in some area of their lives. This is another reason why we must have sober, recovering groups and transparent honesty in our participation; it will help guard us from rationalization, denial, and supporting the illness of others.

We should keep in mind that the question of sexual sobriety goes beyond the question of dreams. Some members have questioned their sobriety or set it back to zero when no sex whatever was involved, when, for example, they lusted after their wife or got drunk on lust. Whether we agree or not, we honor the person's decision, whether they decide for or against resetting their sobriety in such a case. Questions also come from single members who have engaged in heavy physical involvement without the sex act itself. The hangovers of depression, guilt, and remorse tell them, their sponsors, and their groups that something went wrong.

These negative effects are warning signals to stop, look, and listen. Usually, time will tell.

Here again, it is probably best to leave the decision of resetting the sobriety date up to the individual rather than creating some set of rules by which the person will be judged from without. Of course, there may be cases where it is so obvious and the person is in such denial that a sponsor or group may want to confront the person.

We must never forget that the real issue is not some legalistic standing that mere length of sobriety confers upon us, but our *quality of life*. One of the pitfalls of counting length of sobriety is that some may be found who use it as a substitute for the reality of a changed life. Some may be stuck on externals: "I'm sober" equals "I'm okay." *Mere length of sobriety is no more an indicator of recovery than growing old is a sign of increased wisdom.* We can be so obsessed with not wanting to have to set our sobriety date back to zero that we are blind to the reality of our condition. This happens in AA and it happens in SA, but the abuse of the few does not in itself invalidate the value of the sobriety imperative for the many. On the other hand, persons can be so overscrupulous about resetting their sobriety date that they use dreams or other experiences to turn the sobriety imperative into a matter of technicalities, clouding the real issue of recovery.

Those troubled by sexual dreams may do well to ask themselves whether such experiences have opened the door to tolerating lust and increasing their chances of letting it come in and take over. Those whose sex is "unconscious" or "involuntary" may well be cheating themselves of real victory. By trying to push lust down out of sight and put a lid on it, we foster a deadly blindness. If we find ourselves in this place, we can ask for grace and help to see the reality of our situation, come out of denial, and into surrender and freedom.

Members have found that one practical means of progressive victory over sexual dreams is to call another member on the spot, regardless of the hour. Members report being able to condition themselves to waking up immediately. They then call another member and tell what is happening to break any power the experience has over them. Continuing this process whenever temptations occur in sleep makes us accountable to someone, takes us out of hiding with our secrets, and brings increased victory over the problem.

Ever since realizing I can act out my lust in my sleep and that I have the choice not to, I try to remember, each night (and each morning), to surrender all of my lust at *all* levels. I'll say something like this: "I'm powerless over my lust. I don't want *any* part of it, inside or out, conscious or subconscious, active or passive. I send it away. Please keep me sober from it because I can't." And lest fear of falling make me fall, I also acknowledge my powerlessness over that, surrender the fear, and ask Him to take it away too.

The best way I've found to get victory over my lust during sleep is to get victory over the looking and thinking when I'm awake.

As the recovering alcoholics say, "Stinkin' thinkin' leads to drinkin'." It is at the conscious level inside my own head where I find I am powerless and must, through surrender, make the connection with the Source of my life.

My subconscious is *me,* and I need help for *all* of me. If I try to *control* lust, at any level, I only repress it and make things worse. I know that I can, through surrender and working the Steps, slowly learn to give God control over my waking and sleeping thoughts. And what a miracle this is! Why settle for less? Who really wants to be a "dry drunk" when he or she can have the full freedom of a surrendered life?

"Half measures availed us nothing."

30 July 1985, rev. 1/90

Some Thoughts on Sexual Abstinence

Given my own sexaholism and the climate of the times, it's no wonder I had concerns about whether or not I could do without sex. My programming told me that such a thought for a man was simply out of the question. I was confusing sexuality with having to have sex, but these are two completely different things. What I have discovered is that I can be fully male and a fully sexual human being without having sex.

Before sobriety, the more captive to lust and sex I became, the more my sexuality was diminished. Without realizing it, I was actually negating and destroying my sexuality. Now I see that for me, the sexaholic, it was the attitude of mind and heart and my character defects that fueled my "sex drive," rather than masculine necessity.

For myself, I find that going into sexual abstinence in my marriage is a matter of choice. When I decide to do it, I simply "shut down the system" by cutting off the demand and expectation. I imagine myself turning off the gate valve that controls the water main going into our house. As I am doing this, I put my desire for sex into God's hands. In other words, I have planned to shut down, for whatever reasons (hopefully the *right* reasons), and then, when the time has come, I deliberately make the decision to stop having sex. And the system shuts down! Of course, I had to learn to trust the process, and for me that took time and practice.

On the other hand, we should always be careful to examine why and how we are stopping sexual activity. This gets clarified over time, if we are honest, open-minded, and willing to see the truth about ourselves. Sharing with the group and/or sponsor should help us be clear on our motives and willingness. And there's a world of difference between trying to *control* sex by force of willpower and freely giving up the demand and expectation for sex in positive surrender. Repression may not only be harmful, it will preclude the benefits that can accrue from periods of abstinence. The healthy way is to surrender demand at the source – in the mind and heart – out of our own enlightened self-interest and desire.

As the time arrives when I would normally be having sex – whatever expectation is established from the previous habit pattern – sometimes I'll feel the desire knock on the door. My mind is telling me, "It's time to do it." At other times, even this first reminder is absent, and there is no message for sex at all. If that quiet message does knock (thank God it's quiet now; before sobriety it would scream out and have to have its way), I simply don't open the door, and it leaves quietly as it came, without any discomfort. If my original decision to stop is a "maybe," or I'm doing it for some reason other than my own self-interest, when desire knocks on the door, I'm tempted to open it a crack to see what's there, and it gets its foot in the door like a persistent salesman. It's harder to shut the door when that happens. The best way is simply to let go of it freely without any "maybes" and give it up to God and His will, one day at a time.

24 August 1985, rev. 1/90

What About Romance and Passion in Marriage After Sobriety?

I'm grateful to have received your letter and want to try to respond to your dilemma of being unable to have "healthy, normal" sexual relations with your spouse.

This is a very timely question, and one I hope we will take up in our future SA retreats and get-togethers, where we can share our experience on this and other subjects related to recovery and healing in the marriage.

First, be grateful that you *are* able to maintain sexual sobriety! That's good news! Without this, there's no hope of anything! This probably means you are letting God into your life and marriage and SA group. Sobriety is the beginning of a whole new way of life for you and your spouse – something you *will* discover on your own if you stay sober and keep walking in the light. A rewarding adventure, believe me!

The first thing that happens when we get sexually sober, it seems to me, is that we go into a state of shock. This shock is spiritual, emotional, and sexual. It is spiritual

This piece is taken from a letter of January 1986, responding to an SA group inquiry.

shock because we have undergone the most profound change of attitude in our entire lives; we have come to the end of ourselves and turned our will and our lives – including sex – over to God. It is emotional shock because letting go of our drug lets our true defective natures float up to the surface. We begin to see in ourselves and spouses things our drug previously covered over. It is a state of sexual shock because we are undergoing withdrawal from lust, and in many cases, from sex. It is not uncommon for some members to temporarily lose all desire for sex. The shock eventually wears off.

All of this has a deep effect upon the emotional, spiritual, and sexual relations between husband and wife. Sometimes we're so involved in the problem of "relating" we can't see what's going on; we're just reacting to each other. It takes time for these things to become apparent. Never underestimate the changes that are taking place. After all, it is a kind of new birth we are going through; we're leaving one world and entering another, though we seldom realize what's really going on at the time.

This state of affairs with husband and wife, where one or both are recovering from the obsession of lust and sexual addiction, is what prompts many of us to go into a period of sexual abstinence with the spouse's consent. (See the article "Abstinence in Marriage.") We do this for many reasons, discussed in these articles, not the least of which is to begin getting victory over lust lest we carry it into the marriage bed again. During this period of sexual abstinence, we make it a point to increase our nonsexual communication, care, and contact. By taking sex out of the equation, we begin to see what is really in the relationship, and what is not there.

When I became sexually sober and was reunited with my wife, we remained abstinent for several months because of the extreme stresses surrounding the separation. I thank God for that period. Later, a few years into my current sobriety, I saw that I needed another period of abstinence.

It lasted for about six months. This proved to be the best time of our entire marriage to that point. We began to see our underlying sick dependencies. I began to see my wife as a person for the very first time, and I liked what I saw. What I began to see was a person – unique, defective, vulnerable – just like me. And I began to see there *was* a very special bond between us, a bond that I wanted to nurture. But this bond had been masked over by the sexual and emotional dependencies.

Over the years, a transformation has come about. Before sobriety, she was the one who almost always initiated sex. I often resented her for doing so even though I was dependent on this and wanted it. Time and time again, she would want to initiate sex right after I had just had sex with myself or someone else. At other times, if she didn't initiate it, I'd resent her for that too.

There was another process going on in the pre-sobriety phase of our marriage. Consciously and unconsciously, I was programming her to cater to my lust. Of course, I thought it was just good ol' healthy passion. (It takes recovery and time to see lust for what it is.) She picked up on it readily. She got infected by it; she wanted to please me. When I began changing, I started the painful process of becoming independent of her. I *had* to to survive! There would be no growth until *I* cut the umbilical. And she had to slowly learn how to adapt to all of this. We both did, and it took a lot of pain and a lot of time. But it was worth it; this *is* the process of recovery.

And the way we came to have sex reflected our deepening union. Some of the things we had done during sex just fell away over time, at first because they simply became unnecessary, later, because they became undesirable. But always because we were finding the real, the true, and the good.

Today, neither of us has to meet any sexual expectations of the other. And we're very happy about that. She knows I can do without sex, and she seems relieved by that. And we both prefer doing without all that lust-intensity stuff when we do have sex now. We discovered we had each other, that we were bonded to each other apart from lust and sex. What a beautiful freedom! I would never have guessed that was possible.

Today, I am slowly – very slowly – beginning to take up the responsibility I formerly shirked of setting the example for the spiritual lifestyle of our union and family. I am beginning to see what it means to be a male, a man, a husband, and a father. I feel great strength and serenity in building a spiritual rather than physical basis for our union. There could never have been any security based on the physical anyway; she would never have been able to achieve or retain the body my lust fantasies required. Even if she had, it would not have satisfied my lust. It wasn't enough when she had a perfectly youthful figure. Lust always wants more. Now, I'm looking forward to growing old with her, and I find myself realizing that the physical attributes mean less and less each year. As this happens, I discover more and more of the inner person that is there. What an adventure!

What's the key? First, taking lust out of the picture. Then, taking the *demand and necessity* for sex out of the picture. We're discovering in SA that sex, even in marriage, is truly optional – if the attitude toward abstinence is healthy. As we increase the true union of persons, sex becomes an expression of that union, instead of a substitute for it.

Another thing: How can we who were sexually addicted – who did what we did in lust and sex – how can we expect *not* to have problems with sex, romance, and passion? (I discovered there was such a thing as addiction to sex in my sober marriage, and many of us, in addition to being sexually addicted, identify with what is often described as romance and relationship addiction, or both.) Yes, SA husbands and wives do have problems with sex. But we've found we can walk through them and grow. In sobriety, things begin to change. For the better, if we simply allow it.

So we reduce our expectations; they were programmed by a way of thinking and acting out that was unreal. Of course we're going to experience changes in our sexual relations; something would be wrong if we didn't!

You say you feel little or no passion for your mate, and when you do engage in relations you feel very unsatisfied. But just look at what used to "satisfy" us before sobriety. If our spouse didn't provide the stimulation, we conjured it up ourselves or went outside for it. And when they did provide it, it wasn't enough even then; lust always wanted more and different and "better." Do you know how common the phenomenon is among both men and women SA members – imagining they're with others while having sex with a partner? It's practically everyone's story! The infection needs healing, and healing begins by surrendering. The secret is not to want anything. When we give up, we get something better. Another member shares as follows:

> *"The Lord is my Shepherd, I shall not want. . . ."*
> *The phrase "I shall not want" has at least two meanings: I will be given what I need (this is the easier of the two), and I will not want for myself, but will want God's will for me (not so easy).*

Recovery from lust. That's what it will take for any of us to have "healthy, normal sexual relations." Fact of the matter is, we sex drunks probably never did have healthy, normal sexual relations with anybody! We thought we did, but now we're discovering that was not really sex at all. It was an unreal demand we put on sex to fulfill whatever our sickness wanted.

After my wife and I started having sex again in my sobriety, one day I told her about my acting out, trying to make some sort of amends. Fortunately for me, I didn't go into detail, and her response was accepting. (We should be

very careful about these amends – read the caution to newcomers in the SA book.) I was overwhelmed! Later, we had
sex, and it was the first time in my entire life I had sex
without the fantasies, without the scenario of lust in my
head. Without passion and romance. We were one, and the
sexual union flowed *from* the spiritual union. It came out of
her response and my response to her response. Once I experienced that, I knew that what I had been having all my
life was not "normal" sex at all. I had discovered something
better – the real. And I began to see, through our experience, that the real sex was very simple and good, that it
asked for nothing, that it didn't demand anything and came
from the inside out, rather than from the outside in, that it
satisfied.

As someone has wisely said, all images and sensations,
if idolatrously mistaken for Joy itself, soon honestly confess
themselves inadequate. This is just what we are discovering
in our SA recovery.

So, we slowly wean ourselves from what is idolatrous
and learn to love. Not because we know how or want to; because we have to. Once we can discern lust, subtract it from
the equation of sex, and start seeing the true spiritual basis
of our union, we can start giving, for that's what love is.
Love is not a feeling; it's a *decision!* And when sex flows
from this union, it is satisfied. It doesn't need the "romantic
and passionate." Sex between those whose wills and lives
have been turned over to the care of God and who are sexually sober is something one cannot adequately describe. It
is sex without lust and not tied to any addictive need or expectation and coming out of love and healthy union.

The media-saturated world of today is very good at
describing the passion and romance, but it has no handle
whatsoever on the real article. I personally feel the reason
"love" appears to be so sexy and romantic in our artificial
world today is because we no longer have the real thing. If
we had it, we'd be satisfied. But we don't have it, so we're
not satisfied. We have to look, hear, taste, and feel more and

more of the substitutes. That's what was wrong with us sex drunks – we overdosed on "romance and passion" till we couldn't cope with it any more! Unreality stopped working for us. Thank God! Now we can start all over as "adolescents," walk through the painful years of growing up, from which our habit cheated us, discover our mate, and grow *together* into the image and likeness of true manhood and womanhood, into the image and likeness of our God.

In Summary

Marriages in recovery in SA seem to go through initial shock and through a new kind of "adolescence." Things change in sobriety. Be patient; the payoff is one of the most precious things life has to offer.

There's something better than romance and passion – love. But we never knew what it was, and it takes all we've got plus God and each other to discover it. And it takes *time*.

We have to give up our old ideas and let go absolutely to experience the new reality.

Consider trying sexual abstinence in your marriage, and let it be open-ended. Don't put a time limit on it. Talk with others who have gone through it. (Be sure to read the "Abstinence in Marriage" article so your spouse is with you and doesn't feel rejected.)

Be open and willing to see the broader aspects of our malady. Our diseased attitudes toward romance and relationship are part of our sexaholism. These can be just as crippling and destructive as our sexual addiction. Often, our sexual addiction has covered underlying pathology, and sexual sobriety, without recovery in these other areas, is recovery that is incomplete, perhaps even aborted.

30 January 1986, rev. 1/90

Another Look at the Misconnection

The other day at work a woman came by with a small bundle of mail for me. I was sitting at the computer, so she had to reach over the desk to hand it to me. She reached out with a big warm smile that lit up the whole place – and me. As I returned her smile and reached out, I found myself wanting to take, not the mail, but her hand.

I settled for the mail, but began thinking about the experience and did a mental inventory. What was really going on in that transaction? Someone examining it clinically from the outside would doubtless point to it as a normal, healthy response. But I was the only one who could tell what it really was, from the inside. I am not merely the sum of my actions; I am the thoughts and intents of my heart.

What I wanted in that instant was the person herself. I wanted to take her into me, to possess her. It had nothing to do with the body or the hand and wasn't lust as we commonly experience it. It had everything to do with the smile and the offering. Whatever was behind that smile could light up my life, lift me out of myself, give me energy, give me life itself. I wanted to connect with the *life* that was promised. I take your life to give me the life I don't have. The Great Misconnection.

I think what we see here is one of the fundamental characteristics of our sexaholism. *The core of my condition is that I want to connect with another as Source of life,* to use another for an end he or she was not intended to fulfill. Thus, the person or sex object becomes a God-substitute, an idol, and I have perverted my natural instinct.

Don't we all remember those marvelous feelings of the new "light in our lives"? How delicious it was to drink in and savor the person. "You light up my life. . . ." goes a recent popular ballad. And a generation ago, it was, "Drink to me only with thine eyes. . . ."

Had my lust been operating, my response to the outstretched hand would have been to take the hand, and that would have energized me to keep on going for more. But what would the end have been? That glorious electricity of the allure of promised light and life would have only discharged, leaving my soul drained, with less than it had before! And I'd be off and running again!

We're beginning to see what lay behind our acting out. Before sobriety, we opened our soul to the images we were masturbating to and to those with whom we would misconnect: the body and spirit of a man, woman, or child. We drank it in, possessed it, were possessed by it. It was our nourishment and sustenance, the most important thing in our lives. It was an act of worship. We made others serve our unnatural demands.

We're also beginning to see the effects of all this as our continued sobriety uncovers the defective self: Single members, starting to date again, get caught up in the old behavior, trying to "control and enjoy" the old feelings connected with their acting out, asking themselves, "What's wrong? Why can't I handle this?" How easy it is for us to still hang on to our misconnections, even though they may not seem "sexual." Married members begin to discover the depth of the addiction and misplaced dependency *in the relationship.* We all need such healing.

Unless we find a connection with God, recovery eludes us. When we discover a faith that works in surrender, and start learning how to give, we get what we really needed all along; we make the only Connection that "satisfies the longing soul and fills the hungry soul with goodness."

9 April 1986, rev. 1/90

The Joy Response

Once I started staying sober, every lust temptation I had was accompanied by fear. The more of a trigger the image was, the greater the fear. This fear isn't easy to describe; it seems to include fear of woman, fear of man, fear of being overwhelmed, fear of losing control, fear that the first "drink" will light the fuse of desire that will ignite my whole being, fear of unleashing the Monster, fear of shutting out God, fear of the darkness that descends. . . .

When I was first sober, this fear was very intense. I remember saying in meetings time and again, "I feel like I'm walking precariously along a narrow path only as wide as my foot, with a bottomless abyss going straight down on either side. It's the line between life and death, and any minute I can lose my balance, tip over, and keep falling forever into the turbulent blackness." There wasn't much recovery there, but that was all I had.

I didn't realize that coming off sex, lust, and relationships meant that the foundation of my whole existence had been torn away, and there was nothing solid yet to take its place. The very core of my being had no support, nothing to stand on. I felt very, very shaky. All I had was the support I got in meetings, even meetings in which I was extremely uncomfortable. As the years went by, the fear diminished in intensity but was still there. I finally reached a sort of truce where I was no longer afraid of the fear. But it took a lot of sharing in meetings and one-on-one and working the Steps to begin to have even a little feeling of security.

All this time I used various prayers in the moment of temptation: "I'm powerless, please help me!" "I surrender my right to lust." "I don't want any part of this lust." "I send my lust onto You; I don't want to bear any of it." "I want you to bless this person and help them." Etc. It worked, thank God!

Such actions became an immediate reflex, almost automatic. I had come to make peace with my lust. I discovered great freedom in acknowledging what I really am. No more denial or blaming it on others or on stress or circumstance. I am a lustaholic, and it's *my* lust that wants to bust out. It was as though I had come to an understanding that lust would always be there, waiting for an opportunity to be indulged, but that I could respond in surrender—that quiet "dying upward" – and be freed from it by His grace. I was comfortable with the situation. But I began to wonder, then ask, "Is there something better than fear?"

Just recently, I was studying the first few paragraphs of The Letter of James when something struck me. He says, "Count it all joy . . . when you fall into various temptations." It occurred to me that I might try gratitude whenever I was tempted. The next temptation I had happened to be resentment-anger, and as I became aware of it, I thanked God for the situation and for victory over my resentment. Doing that felt strange, but I thanked him for both trial and victory *while feeling resentful*. I was immediately loosed from it. And the feeling that followed was better than what used to accompany the previous deliverances. As victorious as the fear-surrender experiences had been, this was better. The feeling was positive and buoyant, instead of mere relief, and there was something new – joy.

Then I tried this on the next lust temptation. As soon as I thanked him for the victory, the fear dissolved and joy came. So I kept trying it on lust and resentment, and then on fear – my Big Three. And it worked on all of them! And it's still working. *I bring my Rescuer into the temptation with me.*

This is very new for me today, but I like the feeling: acceptance, gratitude, and joy are better than fear. And I'd rather have this than the mood-altering pills I took before sobriety. Real joy, and without a hangover! I'm not naturally a very joyful person, but now I have a way I can actually bring joy into my life – through every temptation and trial!

Whenever I "count it all joy," I *have* joy! What a gift.

2 May 1986

Anatomy of a Look

I was driving home from work. My inner attitude wasn't the greatest. I hadn't shared in last night's meeting as I had needed to; something with my wife was unresolved, but there was nothing drastically wrong. It's just the way things are, sometimes.

Then, there she was. Walking against traffic on the right side of the street. I kept looking straight ahead – sheer habit now most of the time. But in my peripheral vision I noticed that the image might have more to "offer" if I were to look. So why not? Just to see if it's something I shouldn't be looking at. Besides, "I'm far enough along to be able to handle this."

Usually that inner shield is in place – God's presence – the defense against the first look, that which keeps me comfortable and free. Well, for whatever reason, the shield was down, and I took that first glance. Just an eye-blink's worth. The absolute minimum. You know. . . .

This hadn't happened for awhile, and being an isolated example, it caught my attention.

Seeing and looking – what a world of difference for me, the sexaholic! I travel along, letting the imagery impinge on my senses, guiding myself through the streets and ways of my world, just like any of God's other creatures that have eyes, a physical being in a physical world, simply seeing to navigate and enjoy. There *is* beauty and innocence, and I can behold it innocently.

Then, something happens. This natural process changes in an instant. Suddenly, instead of simply seeing, there's a furtive *look*. And I'm a voyeur! A simple lightning flick of the eye; so quick I can say I never really looked. But the polarity changes. Now, instead of light merely coming in, something's going *out!* It's as different from simple seeing as day is from night. Suddenly, I'm peeping out from between closed curtains. A glance *stolen*. Like a spider, darting out in a flash to snare its prey.

In a split second, I'm another kind of being in another kind of world. Reality has shifted. I've opened a window to an inner darkness and let this newly revived creature leap out, snatch, and quickly pull back in. All in the blink of an eye. I've lost my serenity, the light within has gone out, and I feel the old disturbance creeping back – the lust-noise interference. And I'm back in my video world, my secret self, where I can peer out of my soul into the forbidden. (But what's forbidden? It's inside of *me!*)

What's in a look? *I'm* in that look! (Have you ever caught someone else stealing a lust-look?) It exposes me for what I am. It's awesome to see myself looking at that look. This glance reveals the very essence of my condition, the very heart of my malady – our malady. Time and eternity are suspended within this look, matter and spirit, good and evil. My death is in that look. Our whole program lives within this one instant, within this one look. For ours is the Program of the Look.

What is it that's lurking within me always – cunning, baffling, and powerful – waiting for that special moment to flash out and take? ME! The *I* in rebellion against God. That look reminds me of what I really am, and that there's nothing in *me* that can release me from my lust. I am a sexaholic! Through such experiences I see it; I acknowledge it; I accept it. No more denial! I *am* what I am. And God's provision is for me just as I am.

I remember another example of my attitude that day. That same traffic light had "turned against me" again that morning, just as I was accelerating, caused by someone trying to get through the intersection. *I* had to stop! *I*. The Big I. The source of all my troubles. That's what the Look comes out of. "I want; I don't want. I have; I don't have. I, I, I, I, I." No wonder the Shield was down; my ego was up! Ego up, Shield down. Ego up, Shield down, Lust out.

Lust is a function of my ego, just as resentment is. I, the lord of my life – lord over that lust object and over that resentment object – unleash a spiritual force against them both, against their wills, perverting the reality of their person to suit my twisted need. What *is* that negative connection? Why must I keep on making it? So I won't have to look at myself.

I saw it the other way around on my way home from work today. On that same road two teenage girls were crossing ahead of me. One kept automatically flipping her head back as a car approached, expectantly, reaching back with her eyes, as though thinking, Might there be something there for *me?*

"Connect with me and make me whole, we cried with outstretched arms" (and turning heads). Lust for man or woman supremely suits the lust of the ego, for it is the very inner self that is reaching out for connection.

What's in my sexaholic look? It isn't the seeing; it's what I put behind it – the intent. The *Me! I want something out of that look!* That's what alters the reality of what I see. Isn't that where the old Fix, the connection, was always made? The acting out was after the fact. And it's not just the looks; it can be a whole range of thoughts that poke through into consciousness or dreams. They're part of our early warning system, telling us that all is not surrendered. If we're willing to see them for what they really are. That's why ours is preeminently the Program of the Thoughts and Intents of the Heart.

This is the "sound barrier" apparently none of us sexaholics can break: we cannot recover from lust in our own strength. *This* is the point of our powerlessness. That's why so many of us go back out there or challenge the sobriety imperative. *We fear it is impossible to change our hearts.*

There's another part of me the look also revealed, now that I'm in surrender to God. As soon as I began to feel the inner disturbance that lust creates in its wake and felt the loss and darkness descend, just seconds after it happened, I used the tools of the program. Steps One, Two, and Three, all rolled into one telegram to heaven: "I'm absolutely powerless over my lust. I don't want any part of it. I give it up to You. Thank you for this trial, and thank you for the victory!" ("The Joy Response") And within seconds, the light returned, and I was free. *This* is what tells me there is surely a loving God who is with me in the temptation, who delivers and takes away my condemnation. The God of the impossible.

What's in a look? The action-point of our disease, but also the very point of our victory and recovery. In acknowledging our desire to lust, and in surrender, one temptation at a time, we can know our God – the One who raises us from our death and gives us life.

August 1986

Why Relationships Did Not Work for Me as a Sexaholic

But they *did* work! And how they worked! I loved them. I enjoyed them and felt good about them. I needed them. It was free love and new freedom. Each time. A new adventure. The "answer." But then, there would inevitably have to be another.

The "relationships" were of various sorts: casual, committed, engaged (with and without the engagement ring), live-in, live-apart, live far apart, continuous, periodic, on call. From the "innocent and lovely" to the base.

They made me feel better. Having relationships was better than masturbation and prostitutes, I told myself. (Or was it?) And the partners enjoyed it too. (Or did they?) It made me feel alive, connected. (Just like prostitutes did, come to think of it.) As far as having sex was concerned, I appeared to be normal, functional, and healthy – on the outside. Of course there was the dreaded specter of impotence, increasingly haunting every assignation as I blazed ahead on the Broadway of Romance and Relationships. But I didn't want to face those telltale warning signals.

Strangely, the relationships did *not* keep me from masturbating or seeing prostitutes. Relationships seemed different from these other forms of acting out, but I still had the dark side with me. Relationships never fixed me. They never kept me off the other forms of the drug. Looking back, I see they not only masked my condition, they supported it.

No one could have told me there was anything wrong with that way of life for me. "You can't take *this* away from me!" (The same kind of reaction to my mother's gentle admonition to not play with myself when I was a child.) I had to stay in charge; I wanted to "control and enjoy my drinking." To give it up would have meant losing one of the more alluring forms of my drug. It would have threatened my very source of life. I *needed* all those "bottles" stashed here and there – just in case I ran out somewhere along the line.

In recovery, I now see that all of this was living in a two-dimensional world. One whole dimension of my being was shut out in those relationships. They sealed in and reinforced my defective nature; I could not come out into the light. I would have to be changed before I could have true union with anyone, but in that world I could not change!

However, once I stopped acting out sexually in *all* forms, including relationships, and began to have progressive victory over lust, I began to enter a new dimension, a totally new reality.

As I started changing my attitudes toward myself and others, I began acquiring a new set of values. I slowly became a new person, a changed person, a better person; and this process is still going on. Recovery. Inside that old two-dimensional *un*-reality I could never have known what the real was like. How could I? But once I was born into the new life, some very profound changes were taking place that would render the old way of life destructive. That way of life had kept me from myself; it was death to me. I no longer wanted what those "relationships" had to offer. I didn't want to have to pay the price – *inside me.*

I often enclose the word "relationships" in quotes because I challenge anybody, those former partners of mine included, to show me where I was really *relating,* that is, being truly intimate, with anyone. "The primary fact that we fail to recognize is our total inability to form a true partnership with another human being," it says in the *Twelve and Twelve,* Step Four *(page 53).* And if this is true for the alcoholic, how much more so with the sexaholic, whose malady strikes at the very core of his or her relational instincts, attitudes, and behavior?

I had always been *taking,* and usually the partners wanted me for the same reasons I wanted them. Want, want, want. . . . Take, take, take. . . . Me, me, me. . . . Two people playing a game, keeping each other from the reality of life. The very fact I kept marriage out of the picture meant I was shutting something out of my life – truth about myself – and hanging on to something that shouldn't be there – lust and dependency. And by "falling in love" I was shutting love out. Looking back, I see I was using "relationships" to try to control the addiction. And even during my first period in the program, I was using sex with the spouse to help keep me "sober." That was one of the things that kept me from recovery.

How blessed for two persons to know and trust one another at depth. But they must be open to change and betterment before that is possible and before true union can result. And in that old context *I could not change.* I would change partners instead. That's why "Let's get married" ruined the whole thing. For me, the sexaholic, there's a whole universe of difference between "relationships" and marriage.

In sobriety, marriage is a sanctifying force in both our lives. That's why for me relationships worked against recovery. Relationships, as someone has said, are like a spectator sport, whereas marriage is actually *playing the game.* I'm also discovering what someone else has said, that "Marriage is our last, our best chance to grow up." For me, the sexaholic, relationships were either rooted in lust or dependency, or both. They were open-ended; there was always that "out," and we both knew it. We were cheating ourselves from having to stick with it over the years and walk through to victory, true union, love, and song. And God was not there.

In my marriage in sobriety, I progressively acknowledged and did away with every one of the "bottles" I had stashed over the years, even if they existed only in the hiding places of my heart, for each one still owned a piece of me. One by one I gave up the idea of even thinking about resorting to them again. I gave and still give up my need of them to God. (That was a shaky but clean feeling.) Only when I had committed myself to this one person, with no recourse to others, even if it meant being alone, did I begin to see what true union and love were all about and know the freedom for which I had always yearned.

The spouse and children – they are God's gift to me, through all the pain, to the completion of myself as a person and member of the human family. I don't want that other two-dimensional unreality now because *I have something better.* Reality. What I thought was the "good" turned out to be the enemy of the best. And until I let go of what I thought was good for me, God could never have put something better into my hands.

15 September 1986, rev. 1/90

The Top Plate

We may be experiencing something significant in SA. As far as we know, it first took place at the Warm Beach, Washington convention last year [June 7–9, 1985]. In the three instances where it has been put into action so far, it was reported by several to have been the most potent or meaningful experience of the get-together. The reports on the Maryland Marathon and Mid-Western Regional get-togethers state that the most powerful session of the day was when, under example of the leader, those members who chose, *"gave away their top plate."*

What is this "sending away of the top plate"? It was first used as a practical way of working Steps Six and Seven as a group exercise. Think of the spring-loaded plate dispenser in cafeterias and salad bars – a stack of plates whose weight brings the level of the stack down to about counter-level. As the top plate is picked up, the stack rises, exposing the next plate underneath.

There often seems to be one thought, attitude, or behavior in our lives that's standing in the way of further recovery or growth – one sticking point in our wills, one

---

This piece originally appeared in the October 1986 *Essay*. It is included here, in expanded form, because it has proven to be a tool in recovery, both in personal and group experience.

thing we're consciously hanging on to that obstructs, that's holding everything else down. Of course, at first, this was our addiction itself; without picking it up off the stack, so to speak, and dealing with it, we weren't about to go anywhere. It covered what was underneath. Once we got sober though, we could then see and acknowledge the next defect on which we could work the Steps.

Often we discover the next plate to be a particular resentment, dependency, or other form of our drug. Usually these are merely different manifestations of the ego-force that underlies our addiction – the Big I. We're always faced, it seems, with something too precious to let go of, "self-will which has always blocked the entry of God." (*Twelve and Twelve,* Step Three, *page 34)*

> Even the best of us will discover to our dismay that there is always a sticking point, a point at which we say, "No, I can't give this up yet." And we shall often tread on even more dangerous ground when we cry, "This I will *never* give up!" Such is the power of our instincts to overreach themselves. No matter how far we have progressed, desires will always be found which oppose the grace of God. (*Twelve and Twelve,* Step Six, *page 66)*

"I *can't* let it go!" we say. But we are the only ones who can – and do. And when we do, the grace and love and peace of God flood back in and restore us and make us whole and joyous again.

But there must be someone to send them away *to.* That's why we may need some such special experience with each other and the One who has the only remedy for our wrongs, the only One who can bear them. Our experience seems to be validating the very heart of our program – Steps Four through Ten – the forsaking and righting of our wrongs. It seems to be showing us powerfully that whenever we bring out into the light of one another and send away to God such thoughts, attitudes, and behavior, we connect in a very powerful way with the larger presence, and the light then floods into our souls. We are freed, and we are cleansed. That which was in the way is out of the way. The peace of God prevails within and fills our hungry souls with goodness. And, we are one with each other.

In Warm Beach, the light began breaking on an otherwise strained get-together as we sent away our top plates. First, the leader confessed and sent away his fear and resentment toward one of the other members present, not naming him by name. Then, each who felt so moved sent away his or her top plate as we went around the circle. The big breakthrough came when the other member who had had strained feelings sent away his fear and resentment. When he did so, the two embraced and were reconciled, and there was a burst of light and great joy in the room.

October 1986, rev. 10/89

Covetousness – The Idolatry Connection

Recently I spent a few days in a cabin by a popular lake resort, trying to do some writing. I took a whole slew of books and got settled in, expecting to get a lot done, as I had in an isolated cabin up north earlier in the year. But the spirit of this place was different; it had a typical resort kind of feeling about it. Needing a meeting, I found an AA group that first night, right by the lake.

As I entered the room and came to the empty chair at the table – I was a stranger to all five others already seated there – the young woman across the table looked right at me full-face and opened up with this huge welcoming smile that lit up her whole being, wanting to connect. There was that special weakness about the smile that I, the sex drunk, recognized intuitively, the kind of smile my sexaholism wants to give in to, wanting to enter that weakness and smile back on its wave length. But I lowered my eyes and didn't connect, an unbelievable victory for me. I noticed that very quickly, the young woman was back to herself, not trying to relate to me, and the meeting got started. (Moral: The best way to get someone else's radar turned off is not to send any signal in return! Amazing how that works.)

After the leader spoke, the first to share was a woman, sober from alcohol a number of years, who said she was on the verge of either suicide or drinking because she had just broken up with her lover, and that this was a pattern in her life. I followed, identifying as an alcoholic first. Then I shared my relationship addiction story and disclosed my SA identity, describing my history with lust in its various forms. I sensed they were hanging on my every word.

Guess who shared next – that's right, the young woman with the smile. She said she deeply identified with what I had said and opened up in honest, painful sharing. The whole meeting turned out to be more SA than AA, and she later asked for the SA brochure. We all went our ways, perhaps never to meet again. I went to bed grateful that God had kept me sober from my lust, grateful and full of joy for having been able to give instead of take. But that was just the beginning of the incident for me. The next two days were a different matter!

I found that wondrously inviting smile coming back to mind time and time again. Then I'd find myself imagining I was in another meeting with the young woman and we'd be talking beautiful program together. Or we'd go out to lunch after a meeting, and how nice it would feel to be together. Then I imagined dancing with her in the pavilion across the street. Mind you, because sex was not a part of that imagined scene, I did not think I was lusting. Nevertheless I saw and recognized each of these as temptations and surrendered them, each time. Time and time again. But it began to get my attention: Not only were they not going away, they were escalating! I had to reluctantly conclude that I was obsessed with the person.

What was it, I asked, as I started to do a mini-inventory on the situation? If not lust, what was that feeling I wanted to nourish so – the feeling I was tempted with? I concluded that I wanted to become part of that smile – to possess it. To possess the person. The feeling I had was, You make me feel good. You light up my life. You hold great promise of something I need and want. You'll fill up what's lacking; I'll be completed with you. I want *you*. Smile at me again, and let me lose myself in that smile. Now on the face of it, aren't these all natural boy-girl responses? Then what's so wrong about *my* letting them in and nourishing them?

Sharing this in an SA meeting, I groped for a word to describe it. "It had nothing to do with the drool," I said, "yet it's just as deadly for me. What *is* the word?" A day or so later, I was reading in Paul, and the words literally jumped off the page at me. *"Covetousness, which is idolatry."* That was it – covetousness! "I WANT!" Ego-demand again, just like lust. I already have a wife and want another woman. Wife or no wife, I see now what this kind of wanting is. When I make anyone the light of my life, I shut God out. They take the place of God. And that's why it is idolatry.

The power this covetousness has over me is more subtle than raw lust or sexual acting out. It's at the very heart of the *spiritual connection*. The interface between me and that smile is the very interface between me and Person, between me and God. It's the soul-connection, at the deepest core of my being. It's powerful because I'm messing around with the God-connection. There's only one connection that satisfies my spiritual thirst. If I go to any other *to drink,* I'm doing idolatry, making the misconnection, connecting to a false god, a god of my own making. For here again, I've perverted the real into something to suit my *want*.

"The road narrows," they say. Yes. In early sobriety all I could see was the physical aspect of lust, and that takes a continuing miracle to overcome. But the progressive revelation of my inner spiritual condition strikes deeper than I ever imagined. This is a different kind of ball game; it's all-or-nothing! (It's hard for me to watch a film or TV without wanting to covet and become one with that attractive smile or personality.) It's a no-man-can-serve-two-masters kind of thing. The deeper I see into my powerlessness over this spiritual aspect of my sexaholism, the more powerfully I need God. I need a God who not only delivers from temptation but "who satisfies the longing soul and fills the hungry soul with goodness." I need a God who suits my sexaholic dilemma: I'm disconnected, so my disease cries out that I must connect, possess, be *filled* with someone else. I need a God with whom I can be one, on the inside. I have no choice. Either I am united with His personal presence, or I must fill myself with a substitute presence. My nature abhors a vacuum!

But here's the payoff: The more I see of my defective nature, the more I need. And the more I need, the more I cry out for the reality of His presence and the more I receive of His fullness, grace upon grace. God seems to come to me through my defects every time I'm ready to see and be done with them. The Source of my life! What I've really been looking for in all those Life-promising smiles. How can this be, that a sex-lust junkie and misconnection addict like me can know the God who dwells with the one who is of "a humble and contrite spirit"? Thank God for His inexpressible gift!

January 1987, rev. 1/90

Walk, Don't Run

This will be a tough inventory to write. It touches on some things I think I'd rather hang on to than surrender.

Things piled up on me again yesterday. I had saved up all my vacation and personal leave time at work to stretch the year-end holidays into two weeks by myself somewhere to do what I felt was some important writing. But as things worked out, this was the time the new secretary was starting. Plus, the cabin I'd counted on wasn't available, and I was still recovering from a bad bout with viruses, bacteria, and everything they can do to one's sinuses. I found I couldn't cope with one more phone call, question, or decision; things were closing in fast. I was falling apart. You know the feeling, all stressed out. Things closing in on you. Emotional claustrophobia. In short, I'd become a perfect candidate for self-pity and my old standby – escape. Self-pity impressed neither my wife nor the secretary, so the only thing left, naturally, was escape. I had to simply "get outta there!" I had to run.

I did take time to pray for guidance and really thought a trip to the desert would solve everything. I hurriedly packed the car and headed out. I only made it to Mojave before I had to stop and eat, and figured I'd miss all the scenery on the way if I tried to make Death Valley at night. In the back of my mind, however, was *escape,* not desert inspiration, so

56

I quickly located the only movie theatre within twenty-five miles and sat down to get stupefied – junk food and all. I kept waiting for the mood of the film to change, where I didn't have to close my eyes all the time, but it only got more so, so I hopped out of there. I had to escape from the escape for my own good!

By this time I needed a place to sleep and went off to find one. But nature and the result of my frame of mind – guilt, fear, the movie reaction (I always get movie reactions!), not to mention the junk food I was letting into body and soul simultaneously, all conspired to give me a sudden case of out-house hurry – without an out-house in sight! I didn't find one in time, and the unthinkable happened, the first time since my very first day in kindergarten. Now I really had a mess I couldn't cope with! And I was feeling sick. After an embarrassing few minutes and a hasty change in the cold, I was only too glad to escape home. (Everyone should go through that at least once; it's truly a chastening experience. Talk about trying will power, only to learn how powerless you are. . . .)

On the way home on lonely highway 395, I had plenty of time to reflect on what had happened. Escape, even "innocent escape," doesn't work for me any more. Whatever I do, I've got to stay with reality. When that emotional claustrophobia hit, I should have treated it just like a lust, resentment, or fear attack. I should have stopped, looked, and listened to discern where the wrong was in my attitude. Then, I should have changed my attitude toward that onslaught of feeling and sought the one sure Remedy that always works – surrender to God. I could have "gotten away" from my need to escape by just getting by myself in a quiet corner somewhere. "Getting away from it all" doesn't have to mean the other side of the world or losing myself in the quasi-world of images; it can be taking refuge in the One who brings true peace and serenity. It can be simply a quiet talk with someone else. Strange, how once my attitude changed, I was able to do this.

Another thing I hope the experience will help me remember is the spiritual pollution I foul myself with whenever I *open my soul* to something in escape. Some years ago I stopped watching television one day at a time, and have been wrestling with how I use or abuse movies ever since. Many times I have done inventories like this on movies that have shown me clearly that I cannot handle them. It's not based on their content, though that obviously is a factor. I can't handle them simply because of the way I am. I use them for escape! And escape is getting too toxic for me because I get disconnected. I become obsessed with the images, personalities, attitudes, or atmosphere, which invariably shuts out God! Don't ask me why; I can't tell you why. I just know it's true for me, yet I still want to hang on to this one "last" means of "innocent" escape!

(First Step on movies, anyone?)

Lord, help me see that I can walk out of these feelings, even though they seem so devastating; that I don't have to run away. And purify me from my "lust of the eyes" that I may find my rest in Thee, for Thou art my refuge and my strength.

January 1987, rev. 1/90

Lust, Sex, and the Marriage Misconnection

When I got back together with my wife in sobriety, and after the first few months of abstinence, we started having sex again. I didn't realize it, but it was sex driven by lust. We were doing what we'd been doing for twelve years; it was pretty much sex as I'd had it with anyone, various forms and all. And during sex, I was still resorting to fantasy images and memories of others. Strangely enough, this did not immediately lead to acting out with myself or others. But then, I was getting sex regularly, so what did it matter? Was this another form of the drug? I think so. (I was yet to discover how insidious this malady of ours can be, and it took a lot of sobriety to even begin to see it.) Is it any wonder I slipped?

After I slipped, I then recognized and surrendered this form of lust with my wife, a process that took considerable time and surrender. Sex finally became free of those images and memories. What a marvelous victory. That was such a tough and scary threshold to cross, I guess I thought I had arrived; I was on top of the mountain. It turns out it was just a plateau, but altogether necessary for any further recovery or growth.

For various reasons, and for various lengths of time in the sober years that followed, I would go into sexual abstinence. I was either trying to inventory some aspect of the marriage or my dependency, or abstain because sex posed problems for me, the recovering sex drunk. The sickness of our union in the first few years of my sobriety was so great, yet so impossible for me to see, it's a wonder and a gift that we never blew ourselves apart. Sobriety can put an awful strain on marriage!

I was afraid of abstinence at first; I still thought I had to have sex, that somehow I was supposed to have it. Then, the first six-month abstinence proved to be the best-yet time of our entire marriage of some twenty years. I was finally able to realize I could do without sex completely, and, paradoxically, that was when sex became clean and free and good. I thought I was on top of the mountain again.

Something good was happening: As I stopped depending on the sex-connection, I began enhancing my person-connection and my God-connection.

Abstinence and working the principles of the program taught me many other things. The marriage had not only survived without sex, it was better. I began to get fleeting glimpses of my wife as a person in her own right. She began to get stronger. I also began to glimpse the depth of my emotional-spiritual dependency that underlay the sexual. At one point I remember telling her, "If you don't stop mothering me, I'm going to have to leave!" I was beginning to see the defective dependency – call it *mis*-dependency – but still could not see that it was *my* problem, not hers, and that I was the one who had to change. I was beginning to see that *I* was using her to fill the spiritual void.

After a couple of years, we went into longer periods of abstinence. In the meantime, I had been trying to let go of her as completely as I knew how, letting go of control, expectations, and need (very difficult to even recognize, when you're living with the person). At the same time, I was starting to pray for the marriage. And every once in a while, I'd go through an exercise of giving up everything to God: marriage, wife, children, home, house, job, car, books, and, finally, my physical life. Then I'd take back as a loan whatever He chose to give me that day. Truly a cleansing and liberating experience. And once free of my sick need, my wife began becoming emancipated on her own. Abstinence was helping uncover deeper unsoundness in our union so healing and growth could take place.

As the periods of abstinence gradually became freer, with no need or expectation of sex at all, it dawned on me one day that I had been *sexually dependent* all this time in sobriety – lust or no lust. Sexually sober – yet still addicted to sex?

For others, I don't know what this means; but for me the sexaholic, I could use sex in marriage to cover not only the relational pathology but my own personal defects as well. So there were now two dependencies that had come to the light of day and that I was getting progressive victory over: lust and just plain sex itself. What a new freedom this brought! An independence and strength in merely being able to live on my own without either dependency. Freedom I could never even have dreamed of. But this time, I knew better than to think that I had arrived, because along with this new freedom from sexual dependency came a new awareness. I had this sneaking hunch that there was a deeper pathology underneath even this. All along, lust had been covering the sexual dependency, which had in turn been covering another unhealthy dependency. But what was this bottom layer? How could there be more addictive pathology when lust and sex were both out of the picture?

Real easy! My wife was a woman, wasn't she? And Woman for me meant mother, sex-gratifier, servant, confidant, decision maker, life-support system. So I had to commence the long arduous journey of another emancipation, one that would make the first two – from lust and sex – look easy. For this one meant *growing up.*

It turns out we had been taking the place of God in each other's lives and didn't even know it until we both began emancipating ourselves from each other and letting God have first place. We were each doing this in our own ways and hadn't realized it. First, slowly, I had begun to find in the One who was keeping me sober what I had previously been looking for in lust, sex, and dependency. Then she – freed from my lust, then my sexual, then my emotional and spiritual dependency – was being led on her own journey to faith. As I look back on this precious experience of the last couple of years (out of the eleven of my current sobriety), I see it must have started about the time I began hearing her humming and singing hymns to herself. God, joy, and gladness were taking the place of that awful stress and gloom of mere coexistence.

Now, coming in through the back door, are the very things I had let go of ever expecting: my wife's respect – a priceless gift – her total support, her affection. More than I ever gave up wanting is mine now. No, it's not mine at all; it's *ours,* and that's infinitely better.

Now, I've begun trying to bring her into my program, talking with her as I would in a meeting, leading with my weakness. Though I'd been doing it in meetings, I hadn't come out of that isolation with *her.* And most recently, before going off to work, we've begun saying our own version of the Third Step prayer together. And here's a thought: Now that the sexual dependency is gone, I can have what sex was probably meant to be – the simple, the natural, and the good. But now that I don't need it and don't expect it, I don't have to have it at all. Sexual dependency had been taking the place of something better, only we didn't know what that was because we'd never been there.

When I shared this at a meeting recently, an SA member who is single said, "I had problems with SA's idea of no-sex-before-marriage for the recovering sexaholic, but just went along with it. Now, for the first time, I can see why we say that. Now it makes sense."

What I had before was not "committed relationship" but committed dependency – whether with lover or wife. That's why for me, the sexaholic, recovery has to be not only no sex outside marriage, but progressive victory over lust and victory over sexual dependency *in* the marriage. And finally, recovery is severing the emotional-spiritual *mis*connection by being reconciled to the One whose unconditional love I am just beginning to see and trust.

8 April 1987, rev. 1/90

The Invisible Monster

NEWCOMER WALKS INTO SA. Grabs on to the program: "What a marvelous program; I've been waiting for this for twenty years! It was made in heaven, just for me!" Starts attending meetings regularly. Stops the acting out. Feels the power. Gets involved. Becomes a model SA member. Pretty soon, is being asked to lead meetings. May even begin sponsoring people. Other members feel good about having him or her around.

SAME MEMBER SOME TIME LATER. Subtle changes begin. A faint puzzlement clouds the countenance. Confusion stirs under the surface. Perhaps he or she misses a meeting or two, then attends irregularly. Honesty and God-hunger, so attractive at first, begin to fade. They stop letting the light in and revealing the thoughts and intents of their heart. Various symptoms appear: erotic dreams and looking and "drinking" return (maybe they never went away); they start wondering when they can have a "meaningful relationship." Perhaps there's another unsurrendered addiction at work. Whatever. Next thing we know, they're back out there. The pattern is all too familiar; the specifics don't matter. What has happened? Why? What's going on?

When I was an adolescent, through age seventeen or so, I had a recurring nightmare. I would be in a long dark confining tunnel, struggling manfully toward the distant light, knowing that awaiting me there was a huge invisible monster that would consume me as soon as I broke out into the open. Each footstep was forced; I knew I had to come out, but dreaded it with all my being. I would proceed agonizingly along, knowing I had to keep going, only to wake up screaming each time at the awful end. I could never see, hear, or feel whatever that monster was, but it was all-powerful and annihilating.

In the intervening years I've come up with various interpretations of this, but I'd like to use it as a metaphor for what happened to me and seems to be happening to many others in the program. I was one of those whiz-bang fast-starters who came in with a beaming smile and "Wow-what-a-program!" line. And after a year and a half I went back out there and didn't even know what hit me. I "hit the ` wall," as the athletes say, coming to the end of my own resources. Actually, I was up against the invisible monster. Me.

I met the self I'd been running from all my life – my untamed Ego. I think all this was happening at the subconscious level. Intuitively I began to sense that life without my drug was more than I'd bargained for. I was face-to-face with the emptiness that I and others could no longer fill. I sensed that life without Ego was annihilation, for that was my life. I'd never known life without my ego enthroned in the driver's seat. And the wall I was hitting was the prospect of death to my ego. For me to continue in the program, I instinctively knew I'd have to die. But that meant there'd simply be no self left. But I had to have my self! That's all I am, isn't it?

It's an awesome, invisible dilemma we face when we sense the price we must pay for recovery. We can't put our finger on it at the time. It often begins with a general discomfort or feeling of inner pressure and increased anxiety. It makes us want to get away. We have a mass-reaction. It's as though a force will consume or destroy us if we stay.

Usually, it's "I can't stand that person!" Or, "This meeting's going to pot!" Or, simply, "I've just got to get away; I can't go there anymore!" Or, "I've got so many other programs. . . !" Typically we blame this inner distress on other members or on SA itself.

Another symptom of the invisible monster syndrome is when we've never made that breakthrough of self-disclosure – what the AA Big Book calls "a manner of living which demands rigorous honesty." We are seemingly unable to bring the secret inner life to the light. This may be related to another symptom: lack of a true Step One-Two-Three experience. For us to be comfortable staying, the ego must be surrendered. But that's an intolerable alternative many of us proud folk simply cannot face. The result is that regardless of whether we may be an SA "regular," we have never become *part of*. The Ego in isolation is unreachable; the light simply does not penetrate.

The other alternative, of course, is to escape back into our drug again, as many of us do. There's even a third alternative some of us try: stay in SA but assert the ego more instead of less. Many of us have felt this. Many of us in trusted-servant positions try to become "leaders." (And pride in length of calendar sobriety can fuel this ego-drive.) No wonder someone has said, "When people come into SA they start being gods!" (Weren't we always?) Sooner or later we all discover where that leads – no growth, weakening, or disintegration of the group. Equally as dangerous, we can make gods out of other people, as we often seem to do. Then we usually wind up knocking them down, creating a lot of pain for others and ourselves.

When I encountered the monster, I did what so many of us typically do; I failed to see that whenever I am seriously disturbed, the cause of that disturbance lies *within,* regardless of who or what I thought caused it. Ego is the invisible monster – invisible only to ourselves. Ours is the ego-disease. The most pitiful, I believe, are those of us who try to get or stay sober without surrendering the ego. We wind up fighting ourselves. Someone has suggested that the most repulsive and destructive thing in the fellowship is un-surrendered ego.

There's something else here, too. At the same time we come up against the invisible ego-monster, we're coming up against God – the God who makes a claim on us, the claim of surrender and obedience. For coming off the false god of lust or dependency means having to face the true God. Sobriety begins to uncover us and let the Light in. But we would flee this in blind panic. We don't want to see ourselves as we really are; in our heart of hearts we know what we really are. So is the real monster our own un-righteousness? Do we begin to see that the Program is in-compatible with resting in our own right-ness, that we can bring nothing in our own hands? Can this be why we either have to back away or become god?

We may thus come to sense our ultimate need, not just a remedy for our addiction. We need *the* Remedy for the whole self. When I finally came face to face with this, after a year and a half of physical sobriety, I could not make the transition. I could not stand to face the truth about myself. I ran back into the comfortable darkness, only to find that it too was now intolerable! That brought me to the final despair, what I call that "suicidal" violence that must be done to the ego, where finally, all I could do was cast myself on the love of the One who saw my rebellion and yet was there for me still.

Have we fallen prey to the invisible monster? If so, let us walk through the experience to the new level of sur-render we're being called on to make. Above all, let us guard against slipping into the position of those who "keep coming back" only to get support for their illness and feel better about their acting out!

Those of us who have come through this terrifying nightmare can offer compassion and encouragement to any who may face a similar dilemma in their sobriety or in-sobriety. When we died to Self, came to God and the group with nothing in our hands, we were set free. The dark fear of the monster dissolved, and in its place were light and impossible joy.

29 June 1987, rev. 1/90

Of Soda Crackers and Human Nature

L ate last night, I found myself troubled with a vague un-
settledness. As it began to get my attention, I saw that
rather than anxiety, it had a component of anger in it. I had
been wrestling with an issue facing my life and had let my
negative force play around a little inside against someone
who was an easy target. "Righteous indignation" would suit
my frame of mind perfectly.

I tolerated the negative feelings for a while, then had the
impulse to eat something. I was even aware that I was going
to ingest something – anything – to coat those feelings. But
I intentionally disregarded that insight. The question then
became, What to eat? Generally I limit myself to three
meals with nothing in between, so I thought, Well, I'll just
have a swig of orange juice. But then I thought I'd need
something solid to go with it, and soda crackers would be
just the thing. But knowing I'd be tempted to pig-out on the
combination, I settled for crackers only, especially since my
wife had put in a new supply. I could already taste that delicious something that sets fresh crackers apart and the good
feeling it would give me.

I opened the large tin and was undoing the outer plastic
bag when I started debating how many I'd take. My first

impulse was to grab a whole handful of them, but that made it all too apparent that something was wrong here, and I thought I'd better bring God into this thing. That's when it hit me that this was nothing less than rebellion against God. Part of me wanted to pray that I might follow Him even in this, but I quickly covered it and pushed it under. Besides, how could a couple of soda crackers equate to such a colossal event as a person setting himself against God? I compromised: One or two would be less rebellious, so I deliberately went ahead and took them; and there was a broken part of another one in there, so I took that too. Let's be tidy about this thing!

I felt the darkness of my being; it was an evil act, a deliberate turning against God. I still can't quite comprehend how I could experience such a dread lostness in the context of something as "innocent" as two white soda crackers. I felt the separation immediately, and after it got intolerable, finally surrendered and brought the Higher Power back into the picture: "I don't want this condition; I give it up; come be victorious over my rebellion." And – wonder of wonders – there was union restored within, and peace.

I don't think I've ever seen more clearly the deliberate nature of my rebellion. What does this tell me about myself? It's but the last in a continuing series of revelations of who I really am. Some years ago I saw that I was a sexaholic; I admitted that, and it opened the door to recovery. Once that window into my true nature was open, I began to see progressively that I was also a lustaholic, a resentaholic, a judgment-aholic, a fear-aholic, a dependency addict, and so on. In the last year or so I've come to see that lying behind all this is ego – ego in rebellion. All these temptations to sin against myself or someone else would have me turn away from the light of God. But now that I know I have a choice, as in the above example, I see that it's nothing less than my rebellion. Against God. Ego, someone has said, is edging God out. For me with the crackers last night it was more like elbowing God out. The ego in rebellion is the driving force behind my lust, resentment, judging spirit, self-glorification, fear, and often, it would appear, my abuse of food.

This is incredible! Even now I wonder how such "silly little things" as thinking negative thoughts against people or eating compulsively can possibly be manifestations of such a cosmic act as persons setting themselves against God. My educated mind doesn't want to accept it, but in my heart I know it's true; the incident with the crackers last night proves it. It also tells me that insofar as the inner man is concerned, I delight to do God's will, but there is in my being a different principle which wages war against this and makes me a prisoner of the principle of wrong within me. Underneath it all, I'm a rebel against God. Lust of whatever expression is, for me, a negative spiritual act. The lust of the flesh, the lust of the eyes, and the lust of the ego – this is what constitutes my "world" of living against God.

What is a very sobering thought is that in this very core of my will and being I can be making decisions against God while at other levels I can be going through all kinds of religious or Program motions and sentiments. I see more and more that what I really am is what I am in my secret heart toward others and God.

Another thought: It was my attitude behind the eating that made the eating itself a problem. I can get all caught up in legalistic self-control, an obsession all its own. There's no freedom working only on externals, just greater bondage. Freedom is an inside job, a transaction between me and my God. The real job is cleansing the *inside* of the cup. Physical sobriety – mere length of calendar sobriety – is not an end in itself but a means toward that end.

This cracker incident has turned into a good experience for me. As I see this latest revelation of what I am, I have the same feeling of relief that has come with the other discoveries of my defective self. *All* of my grace comes from above. Rather than giving me less confidence, this gives me more. I see that all of my confidence against slipping and for relating to God has to be based on *God's* provision, love, and care for me, not on my ability to stay sober or be "good."

7 August 1987, rev. 1/90

Sobriety Versus Recovery

I've been going through a grueling exercise lately – reading through a pile of notebooks full of old personal notes, memoirs, and inventories from my first entrance into the program, over thirteen years ago. This material was hitting me so powerfully I decided to look at it critically and ask what it told me about myself. I was shocked. Mind you, this is all material written *after* I entered the program.

First, I can't believe how obsessed I was with myself. I was almost always thinking and writing about myself: *my* job, *my* career, *my* marriage, *my* problems, *my* sex life. No wonder I had so much inner conflict and pain; I was full of myself! It's so obvious, looking back on it all from a great distance; it's like reading someone else's story. I could also see some of the self-deception and blindness – large at first, slowly diminishing as time went on.

How slow recovery is, and how slowly the program works, even when we're working it. "Two steps forward and one step back," as the saying goes. It was disturbing and painful to see myself revealed in those notes, but I could also see that God was working through it all, both to will and work for His good pleasure. There was a unifying

---

This and the following two pieces were originally written as one in November 1987 under the title "Sobriety or Recovery? – The False-Recovery Syndrome."

force at work instead of the disintegration so evident in the preceding years, and there was finally direction in my life – the right direction. What an amazing grace! I'd like to share part of what I discovered as it bears on the concept of what recovery is and what gets in its way. Sobriety (in the narrow sense) and recovery are two different things.

The biggest shock was looking back at my old attitude toward sex in my marriage. Two and one-half years into the program I still had the idea that sex with my wife was going to help keep me sober, and if we'd just have more sex, all those nasty (delicious?) old memories wouldn't keep coming back! There's no more glaring illustration of my blocking my own recovery than this matter of sex with my wife; first, carrying lust over into it, then, after that was surrendered, the sheer habit of sex with her. Reading those on-the-spot notes of mine led me to conclude I was addicted to sex while I was sober! How can this be? Very simple: *I had to have it*. It wasn't biological necessity; it was, "I gotta have it!" This attitude for any addict is dangerous; and when the sex addict says he's got to have sex, watch out!

The thing that hit me next in this look into my past was how prevalent and pervasive lust was, parading in different guises. (Of course, it's easier to see it, looking back on it from a distance; that's why we need meetings and association with mature sobriety and recovery.) From day-one sobriety on, although I may not have recognized it as such, I was wrestling with lust in many and various forms. For example, I was puzzled why I was tempted with images during marital sex and over some of my other behavior. I apparently didn't make the connection between those problems and flirting with temptation by associating with sexually promiscuous people, especially in other Twelve-Step program meetings. Why was I still gravitating toward all that stuff on display and within such easy reach?

Two things brought progressive victory over lust from that point on. The first was letting sex become optional instead of mandatory. (I gave up the demand and right to have sex in the marriage.) This took some doing; it didn't happen all at once. It took a lot of work with Steps One through Twelve, and a lot of time. I learned through trial and error first that it was actually possible to live without sex, then, that sex was covering underlying pathology in me and in the marriage that only abstinence would uncover. The intervening years saw a succession of periods of abstinence from marital sex for various reasons, and I gradually came to believe and trust the value of releasing all demand and expectation for sex *and affection,* with no time limit, a process of joyful discovery that's still going on. In this new context, sex, when it happens, is simple and good – no big deal – totally optional. This brought a new freedom, not only in the marriage, but in increased victory over lust.

The second thing that brought increased victory over lust was carrying the message in my own personal Twelfth Step work. I discovered an amazing thing: The turning point in my journals concerning wrestling with lusts, fantasies, infatuations, potential new partners, and that whole business, came in late 1978 and early 1979 (three years sober) when I stopped thinking, wishing, and praying about carrying the message to those who were still sick and started taking the actions. When I launched out into serious Twelfth Step work, lust became less of a problem. I was still inhibiting *recovery* before the Twelfth Step was a reality in my experience. I have the feeling that there is no such thing as solitary *recovery.*

26 January 1988, rev. 1/90

Obstacles to Recovery

Listed below are some inhibitors to recovery garnered from my own experiences and those of others. The list grows as recovery continues.

Hanging on to One or More Forms of Overt Sexual Expression

Many of us identify here. We experiment with how much we can get away with, backing away from our hell, kicking and screaming. I hung on to lust in the marriage bed, either physically or in the mind. From early on, I had never known sex without lust. Once I was aware of what was going on, it took a long time for me to surrender it completely. Other forms of hanging on include: cruising; trying to connect; making connections then backing away, even in meetings; the look drinks; teasing one's self but not to orgasm; physical encounters or relationships without orgasm; deliberate sex during sleep. The variations are endless. If one were invisibly perched on our shoulder for awhile, one would come to see the real addiction in action.

No Progress in Victory over Lust

In the beginning, I was pretty much satisfied with merely not acting out; after initial withdrawal, physical sobriety proved to be no big deal. The focus was on externals; the outside of the cup looked clean, but the inside was full of all kinds of pollution, hanging on to sexual or romantic fantasies, for example. I wasn't as aware of the different guises lust took as I am now. Progressive victory over lust is our aim, but if we fall into the trap of *no* progress, we defeat recovery. If one could slip inside our mind and read our thoughts, one would know our true condition.

Resorting to Other Addictions

In the first years, the other addictions I resorted to (without realizing it at the time) were resentment, television, and marital sex. I include resentment as a true addiction because I was consistently resorting to it as a perversion of the reality of others and mood-altering experience to keep me from seeing myself. Yes, being in bondage to resentment blocked my recovery. I've talked elsewhere about how I discovered I was addicted to marital sex. And as for television, after years of agonizing over it, I concluded I could not handle the impact it had on me; plus, I used it as a drug and for escape. It held me under its power, and the price of losing the Presence became increasingly unacceptable. So I put it down and began working the Steps on it. In the past year I've reluctantly been coming to the same conclusion about my relation to movies. Many members say that progressive recovery has led them to examine their use or abuse of other substances and behaviors.

Lack of Honesty About the Self

In the first few years, I was apparently one of those who were "incapable of being honest with themselves" and who did not grasp and develop "a manner of living which demands rigorous honesty." This failure to "walk in the light" is self-blindness. We fail to get into the practice of that progressive revelation of the self in sharing the thoughts and intents of our hearts in meetings; or if we do, it's not done in surrender and reliance on God but is a kind of mechanical false-honesty that appears to be oh, so honest, yet comes from some other motivation and does not lead to character *change*, perhaps that dumping kind of "honesty," where God and surrender are not present.

Incomplete Surrender

Half-measures. For example, being in the program with a goal such as getting into a relationship or getting married or having sex again. Prior demands placed on recovery short-circuit the healing force of the Steps and shunt us off to the side onto a false-recovery track. "Half-measures availed us nothing." We've never broken through the "Thy-will-not-mine-be-done" barrier. Recovery does not seem to result from trying to strike bargains.

Emotional Dependency in the Marriage

Emancipation hasn't taken place yet; the sexual and emotional umbilical is still connected to the spouse. My story! This may especially be true if we've been in the marriage a long time before sobriety. Such dependency keeps us from seeing the true nature of our defective self and defective relationships as much as hanging on to some other addiction does. Sobriety or no sobriety, the marital relationship itself is often an addictive relationship (addiction to sex or dependency, for example). False comfort prevails – playing the same roles in the same old tiresome game.

Emotional Dependency in Nonsexual Relationships

The same applies here, as in marriage. Those various connections with a former or potential or fantasy lover, for example. The nonsexual dependency is where we experience the addiction in its essential form and see the awesome power it has over us. Ask a member going through relationship withdrawal! That's why so many of us come to feel that the essence of our malady is not sexual but spiritual, immeasurably more powerful than the physical, though not as obvious. "Please connect with me and make me whole. . . ." This is where some of us come to see the insidious power of what some of us call our romance or relationship addictions.

Controlling the Externals

I had a sign above my desk in college: Self Denial For Success. Do you see the fallacy? If I can just control more aspects of the externals in my life, it will give me control over *me*. Some of us can get so inspired by this type of false recovery that the lengths we go to maintain this control will make your head spin. And if we fail, we tighten up our resolve all the more and say, This time I'm going to add such-and-such to my list of no-nos. We appear as admirable examples of tough moral fiber. The visual drinks are timed with a stop watch. We become self-styled paragons of Spartan physical discipline. *We* manage the game in one area of our lives after another until we think we've got all the bases covered – (there's always that blind spot though, isn't there?). Then we come to the sad realization that it's been ego all along, and not a Step-inspired spiritual awakening.

At fellowship level, it's the ego takeover: "I'll control this person or group or situation, and that means I have control over *me*." When this attitude gets into positions of leadership, it can infuse its spirit and ego-force into the fellowship and shape that fellowship to its own image, whether at the group, intergroup, or fellowship-wide level. And yes, it works against true recovery, keeping us from the real thing, because it shuts God and others out and puts Self in the driver's seat.

Not Finding What We Were Really Looking for in Our Addiction

True recovery changes me – slowly but surely. Changing

me changes my view of reality. That old willful perversion of reality begins to change. Thus, inevitably, I should come to see myself, others, and God in a different light than before. I couldn't get into or stay in recovery with my old way of looking at others; and surrendering my resentment and negative force began to change that perception. Now I also wonder if we can be in true recovery with our old idea of the Higher Power remaining as it was. Wasn't that our supreme distortion of reality – the way we conceived of God? I may have professed to believe in God, but He turns out to have been a combination Santa Claus, magician, super-physician, and parent-figure, even though I used religious terminology. You could never have told me I was resorting to a false god of my own making. Now, better able to see the depths of my defective self, I begin to know Him in a way impossible before. Recovery is coming to an increasing Connection with the Source of our lives in a very personal way. We *can* find what lust was really looking for.

Summary

If we are honest with ourselves, most of us will identify with any number of these inhibitors to recovery and will also see them in others. We may well ask ourselves whether any of these inhibitors to recovery have locked us into *false* recovery. Do we judge or condemn one another? No. We thank God for being with us to show us these things and lead us lovingly into the light. We examine ourselves, give up the false, and press on to the true.

26 January 1988, rev. 1/90

How Sobriety Was Keeping Me from Recovery

My first unsuccessful journey into recovery taught me something I'd like to pass on. Mere sobriety in my first one and one-half years was keeping me from experiencing the reality of the Twelve Steps in recovery.

Being technically sober, I came to feel I wasn't really powerless anymore, so the reality of the First Step never stuck. I had never come to terms with the First Step *on the inside;* I had only felt it initially in withdrawal from the compulsion. *Without the continuing First Step experience, there is no Program.* Today I see that I am powerless over lust and a whole lot of other things – resentment and fear, for example. In short, I am powerless over my defective self. Although I had "taken" the First Step many times, there was no continuing Step One reality in my experience.

Without seeing my true condition, how could I come to believe or turn my will and life over to the care of God? Why should I? I'm doing fine! Going to meetings, learning all about the program, getting my chips and birthday cakes. . . . Thus, though I prayed often for help, there was no Steps Two and Three reality in my experience.

Without that continuing honesty about my true powerlessness over self and surrender to God, how could I truly do a fearless and searching moral inventory or see and send away my defects? Steps Four through Seven had not become my new attitude and way of life.

If I wasn't able to see the truth about my defects, how could I properly see where I had wronged others and make things right? I was still pointing the finger at others. Steps Eight through Ten were only a mechanical, sometime thing, not a continuing reality in my experience.

I can pursue all kinds of religious exercises – pray and meditate up a storm! – but there's no true *union* with God when all that unseen garbage is still in the way. No Step Eleven reality.

And I can carry a message all right – the message of my true spiritual condition; that's the only message any of us ever carries. But what is it, and what will it be saying? There was a time when the only message I was carrying was false recovery – a curse to those receiving it. No Step Twelve reality.

Recovery is not "addiction to meetings and socialized spirituality."

Sobriety is stopping; recovery is starting. Recovery *begins* with sexual sobriety; there's no true recovery without it. If the entire history of SA has told us anything, it has told us that with sexaholism, recovery must go deeper than mere sobriety, for ours is the disorder of the thoughts and intents of the heart.

Recovery is the continuing reality of the Steps in personal experience. Recovery is the progressive realization of our powerlessness and dependence on God. Recovery looks deeply into the moral self to see the wrongs and takes steps to surrender them and make them right where any others are involved. Recovery seeks the true worship of God and the true good of others. Recovery results in increasingly true union with others.

Recovery is *discovery:*
　　Of sobriety
　　Of life with progressive victory over lust
　　Of the defective self
　　Of God the Remedy and Lifegiver
　　Of others
　　Of love in the giving.

Recovery is having the spiritual hunger satisfied.

Recovery is life – reproducing, and reproducing reproducers.

Recovery is a spiritual awakening. It says so in Step Twelve: *"Having had a spiritual awakening as the result of these Steps ..."*

January 1988, rev. 1/90

The Picture-Woman Response

In the last year or so of sobriety, I've been looking at my reactions to attractive women. What is this demand that seems to be placed on me every time one enters my circle of nearness? Why do I feel that inner tension? I can understand my reactions when lust was active; there was a potential "fix" out there or there was fear of being overcome by temptation. But why is there still a strong reaction when I'm sober and able to surrender; just what is this disturbance that comes in? Many of us seem to identify with this.

Lately I had been trying to see if my mother connection in childhood and adolescence was the primary agent in this reaction. Wasn't mother there, invisibly between me and every attractive woman? I simply assumed this must be so in my case, it made such good psychological sense. Then, standing waiting for a bus at the airport recently, something else seemed to click. There I was, waiting anonymously amid the flux of travelers – an observer – and I saw myself reacting to the attractive women that passed by or stood near. Matter of fact, *every* woman is automatically evaluated for that *x*-factor. I started thinking about what might be going on in my deep self.

My first thought was, Well, there's mother in there somewhere, I suppose. And I accepted that. But it didn't jibe; there had to be more to it than that. Then something dawned on me: Picture-women. My reaction to attractive women could be the result of what I had programmed into myself since the first time I had masturbated to the picture of one.

Look at the real situation: There I was, from the age of eight on, burning into the neurons of my formative sexual and emotional being picture after picture of attractive women – thousands of them! – each one posed for maximum attraction. Each one *posed for me!* Sex, my most intense, all-involving physical-emotional-spiritual experience, was associated with and fueled by images of attractive women who looked like they wanted me. And truly, each pose seemed designed to look as *attract*-ive as possible. The image the model presented to the camera – to me – was one of a woman smiling at *me,* offering herself to *me,* and wanting *me*. And as the spirit of the age and state of the lust art progressed, the poses more and more were those of someone wanting me to lust after *them,* and beyond that to inviting ever more sordid forms of lust. On and on. . . There's no end to it; lust never satisfies and always demands more. (Even cars are designed to look more attractive every year; lust isn't limited to selling sex objects. But are they really more attractive? I always wondered why, whenever a new women's fashion came out that I thought was *un*attractive, after a certain amount of media exposure, those very same clodhoppers, for example, became lust triggers for me. Which has to tell us something about our human nature, if we stop and think about it.)

Thus, all this programming of a lifetime was burning in the suggestion that attractive women want me and are asking for my attention and lust. (See how this also feeds our ego and insanity?) And since, as far as lust is concerned, a picture woman and a real woman are the same, I'm conditioned to respond to an attractive woman in the flesh the same way I did to pictures. As a matter of fact, the tragic thing for the sexaholic is that neither picture nor person is real; lust perverts both to serve its sick demands. Lust suppresses the truth, the reality, of either picture or person, and lust itself becomes the object of worship, if we can only see it. *My sexaholism can only exist in a perversion of reality.*

Of course, it's all a lie: All attractive women are *not* offering themselves to me, but my programming of thirty-nine years tells me it is so, and my subconscious emotional self believes it – it *has* to believe it. No wonder I still have strong reactions when encountering an attractive woman even though I'm not lusting after them today!

Funny thing; with all this new insight into my reaction to attrative women, I haven't noticed much change in that reaction! All this neat knowledge I've just discovered doesn't give me power to change. What works is God. I bring Him into my lust, weakness, and powerlessness – right on the spot – and instead of retreating inward, I step out valiantly in His strength and give it away to Him.

Recently I became aware of this tension in an SA meeting where one of the women was an attractive newcomer, dressed in such a manner that makes many sexaholics feel very uneasy. I could feel the tension in the other men also. Close encounters! I decided I should "lean into my fear" and bring it to the light, so I shared with the women and the rest of the group something of what I have just described in the paragraphs above, in general terms, of course, so as not to call attention to anyone. As I looked the women in the eyes, leading with the truth of my weakness, I felt all tension vanish. I was absolutely free and clear and could enjoy the rest of the meeting. I had come up out of that dark well of a hiding place, had faced the rampaging wild elephant of my fear, and witnessed it dissolve into light and joy. The false reality of that old conditioned response gave way to the higher reality of what was really there in that room. The tension in the newcomer seemed to ease, and the group was more relaxed after I spoke the truth of where I was. What a marvelous experience.

What's the principle here? We can, through sobriety and working the principles of our program, transcend our conditioning and victimization. Yes, *victory over conditioned behavior.* Thank God! And we don't have to have it all analyzed out. And what a blessed release to be able to come out of hiding and face our fears.

14 April 1988, rev. 1/90

The Reality Perversion

Get in touch with your feelings!" I used to take great delight in how mind-expanding it felt to turn loose my feelings in group therapy sessions. (Now I see it was ego-expanding.) Now, sober and in recovery, I'm beginning to distrust those old feelings; they're too much subject to this spiritual illness of mine. Distrusting my feelings regarding lust, romance, and attraction between the sexes put me onto this caution. I now perceive that my other feelings about people – resentment, fear, jealousy, judgmentalism – are likewise perverted. The Lie is at work in these feelings too. How could it be otherwise? How can I be so totally subject to the propaganda of my lower self in one area (how I perceive a woman or a man) and be immune to it in others? I'm coming to a cautious distrust of such perceptions and feelings.

Let me share a couple of the whopping misperceptions of reality my recovery has already unearthed. These have to do with the light in which I perceived my brother and my mother. Under professional care before the program, I had learned to reach back and try to find the origins and causes of my neurotic thinking and behavior. It sounded so easy: the influence of my father's death, my brother's rejection, and my mother's neuroses and controlling behavior were textbook clear.

I discovered I was a victim. This reinforced my need to blame others for my problems. I could see how my brother (my father substitute) kept negating me and how my mother had suppressed open inquiry and had been so utterly controlling of my life. And so forth. But if others truly were the *cause* of my condition, how could *I* ever be free? I can never change what happened back then. I'd still be on the endless chase after deeper insights into the deeper "causes" of my condition. However, if it's my *attitude toward* life and those people that causes me the real damage inside, then I *can* do something about my condition.

The slow process of recovery has shown me a different reality than the one those old feelings supported. I came to see, through working the Steps and practicing forgiveness, that my brother's reaction to me was one of protecting himself from my sick dependency, that he was actually doing me a favor! Sure he had his problems and did wrong, but he wasn't the *cause* of my bad feelings and behavior and hard luck at all; my diseased attitudes were. Likewise with my mother. In rehearsing the past as seen through my diseased self, I had been looking for things to support my need to judge and reject these people, to find fault with them – all to protect me from seeing the wrong that was within me. What a difference in the perception of reality a change of attitude makes!

The same perversion of reality takes place today – whenever I let it. In rehearsing the last negative incident with my wife or another SA member, for example, I find myself going over it in my mind, pulling out the things I want to hang on to to support my need to reject, resent, or punish. Much as a lens filter lets only certain wavelengths of light into a camera, I filter all the data so that only those details appear that support my case. Sure there may be wrong in what that person did, but my perception of that wrong suits whatever bad attitudes I choose to harbor against them. I choose to isolate the wrong and pervert it, much as I used to isolate various aspects of the image of a woman and pervert them into serving my sick need during masturbation or intercourse. And isolating the wrong in this way pulls it out as a thing in itself; all I'm looking at is that one little action or word, whereas in reality, there's a whole person out there and a multiplicity of life surrounding that one detail. In this sense, the wrong *as I choose to harbor it* is not real; I give it soul and substance in my thoughts. Instead of expressing the truth of my feelings honestly on the spot, I let the anger, for example, *into me,* getting a hit off it and letting the resentment poison *me*.

My lust creates the wrong: My sex-lust creates the misperception of the reality of woman, and my resentment-lust or judging-lust creates the misperception of anyone it happens to focus on negatively. What an awesome power I have within me to distort reality, to destroy the good, the true, and the beautiful! No wonder they call it insanity.

The amazing thing is that whenever I see and surrender *my* wrong attitude, not only does my disturbance cease, but my perception of the other person seems to change. When I stop playing judge, I can let go of the wrong and I'm free of it, instead of being obsessed by it. And when I take the action of love to reach out of myself and reconnect with that person, it completes the circle back into reality. God is the key, even here. When I yield my will to the Higher will, the true balance of my nature is restored, within and without.

16 April 1988, rev. 10/89

The SA Misconnection

At the heart of our condition is the drive for true union with Person. Bonding. This drive, instead of having been diminished by our misconnections in lust and sex, seemed to increase. Never satisfied with the substitutes, our longing for personal union merely deepened and energized the vain pursuit for the real.

We come into SA, come off the substitute connections, and, lo and behold, we start finding true union with person in other SA members. First, as we identify with them in meetings, sharing honestly. There is oneness here; the first time we've ever been intimate with people in the deepest secrets of the heart. We are totally exposed and vulnerable, leading with our weakness. And we are accepted! And the others feel the same way. The "safe haven" of being together is a marvelous refuge. A dependency develops; we need them coming back to meetings, and they need us. We sense that the whole is greater than the sum of its parts, and that we must continue having whatever it is we're getting there. Fellowship. That's why it's so threatening for regulars to stop coming to meetings.

Then, we may single out those toward whom we have some special affinity, for whatever reason, and risk closer intimacy. More self-disclosure and more intimacy ensue. But something else happens. We also begin to see their defective natures in action. And they ours. Often, we don't like what we see, or how we are seen, and our impulse is to push them away or to back away ourselves. They're part of true union now; they've got to be perfect! They *can't* let us down. Thus, we bring to this growing interaction and union all of the faulty mechanisms of our sexaholism, *for ours is the illness of misconnections.* What happens? The very people we need so desperately for recovery – other members – eventually begin relating to us out of their sickness! And we out of ours. How can it be otherwise, given what we are? Sometimes it's such a jolt we don't know what hit us. Pain.

Because one essential aspect of our malady seems to be misplaced dependency, we often unwittingly make the other person serve more than his or her natural place in our support system within the fellowship bond. Love and support stop being enough. Perhaps we need them too much, as we did our parents or lust or dependency objects. Perhaps they need us too much. Perhaps we begin transferring suppressed anger at parents or authority figures onto them, or they onto us. Maybe it's sibling rivalry all over again. *All of the relational dysfunctions with which we come into SA eventually get expressed in our relations with other members.* When this happens, it's just a matter of time before that person "lets us down," just like we thought everyone else used to do, or when they no longer "satisfy" our need of them. All this can blow us apart, and sometimes does.

Thus, the very mechanism of our addiction can come into play between SA members. We can act out our sexaholism with each other without having sex or lust! *That's why victory over our dysfunctional relations must become part of the process of recovery.* We'll never get well without it. We learn to simply trudge through the pain and learn from experience. The Steps and Traditions tell us how. And we can walk through the experiences to build a deeper bond.

When The Misconnection threatens, one response we can take is, instead of fighting back or running, to humble ourselves before God, accept the situation, and pray that we might be free of resentment. Then, we can ask that we might be able to relate to that person in accordance with *God's* will and not our own. And we can start praying earnestly for God to bless that person as we leave the future of the relationship in His hands. The result can be a growing ability to relate to that person and others in genuine friendship. If we do not get the results we hope for, we leave the other person in God's hands. In any case, we find that *we* are healed and are able to relate better with others. None of this is easy, but we can do all things through Him who strengthens us.

This points up the necessity of making the transition to our true Connection with God as soon as possible. If we linger on having the group, sponsor, or other individuals as our higher power, they may remain nothing more than a power created in the image of our own sick need. A *lower* power. Which prevents our real need from ever being filled. Without finding personal union with God in our own experience (The Twelve Steps), we increasingly must use, abuse, and distort other relationships in attempts to fill that need. This basic need of ours – personal union with God – won't go away; we've got to have some kind of connection. That's just the way we are.

It seems we can't survive in the fellowship we need for survival without learning how to love one another *through the pain and illness*. And considering the load of liabilities we come in with, we don't seem to be able to love without the love of God. In the final analysis, our program always seems to come back to God and His love for us. We can and do love, because He first loved us.

October 1988, rev. 1/90

A Vision for You

We realize we know only a little. God will constantly disclose more to you and to us. Ask Him in your morning meditation what you can do each day for the man who is still sick. The answers will come, if your own house is in order. But obviously you cannot transmit something you haven't got. See to it that your relationship with Him is right, and great events will come to pass for you and countless others. This is the Great Fact for us.

Abandon yourself to God as you understand God. Admit your faults to Him and to your fellows. Clear away the wreckage of your past. Give freely of what you find and join us. We shall be with you in the Fellowship of The Spirit, and you will surely meet some of us as you trudge the Road of Happy Destiny.

May God bless you and keep you – until then.

SEXAHOLICS ANONYMOUS is a fellowship of men and women who share their experience, strength, and hope with each other that they may solve their common problem and help others to recover.

The only requirement for membership is a desire to stop lusting and become sexually sober. There are no dues or fees for SA membership; we are self-supporting through our own contributions.

SA is not allied with any sect, denomination, politics, organization, or institution; does not wish to engage in any controversy; neither endorses nor opposes any causes.

Our primary purpose is to stay sexually sober and help others to achieve sexual sobriety. *

Sexaholics Anonymous is a recovery program based on the principles of Alcoholics Anonymous and received permission from AA to use its Twelve Steps and Twelve Traditions in 1979.

* Adapted with permission from The AA Grapevine, Inc.

For more information about SA, write:
SA
P.O. Box 3565
Brentwood, TN 37024-3565

Phone: 615-370-6062
FAX: 615-370-0882
e-mail: saico@sa.org

This book and the book *Sexaholics Anonymous*
are also available on CD and audio tape.
These and all other SA literature may be ordered from
the SA website at
www.sa.org